LIBERIA

Patricia Levy

MARSHALL CAVENDISH
New York • London • Sydney

Reference edition published 1998 by
Marshall Cavendish Corporation
99 White Plains Road
Tarrytown
New York 10591

© Times Editions Pte Ltd 1998

Originated and designed by
Times Books International, an imprint of
Times Editions Pte Ltd

Printed in Singapore

Library of Congress Cataloging-in-Publication Data:

Levy, Patricia, 1951–
     Liberia / Patricia Levy.
        p. cm.—(Cultures of the World)
     Includes bibliographical references and index.
     Summary: Describes the geography, history, government,
economy, people, lifestyle, religion, language, arts, leisure,
festivals, and food of the West African nation of Liberia.
     ISBN 0-7614-0810-X (library binding)
     1. Liberia—Juvenile literature. [1. Liberia] I. Title.
II. Series.
DT624.L48   1998
966.62—dc21   97–43613
                    CIP
                    AC

INTRODUCTION

LIBERIA, AN INDEPENDENT REPUBLIC on the west coast of Africa, derives its name from the Latin word *liber*, meaning free. Its foundation in 1822 as a home for emancipated black slaves from the United States bears noble testimony to its name and its motto: "The love of liberty brought us here." For many of the turbulent years of Africa's history, Liberia stood out as an oasis of stability and peace. However, its recent past has been fraught with problems, with a seven-year civil war finally coming to an end in 1997. Liberia has a fascinating and powerful mixture of Western and African cultures. Its people have undergone terrible ordeals in recent years, but Liberians are now emerging from the troubled times with a new commitment to peace and progress. This book in the *Cultures of the World* series celebrates its new beginning.

CONTENTS

Liberians are an open-hearted and warm people, despite the hardships they have undergone in recent years.

3 INTRODUCTION

7 GEOGRAPHY
Rivers • Coastal lowlands • Hills and plateaus • Climate • Wildlife • Plant life

19 HISTORY
Early History • Founding a country • Money problems • National recovery • World War II • Peace before the storm • Civil war • Peace at last?

31 GOVERNMENT
The True Whigs • The Council of State • Local government • Local chiefs • Systems of justice

39 ECONOMY
The legacy of war • Natural resources • Farming • Transportation

47 LIBERIANS
Demographics • The tribes • The Americo-Liberians • Others • National dress • Some famous Liberians

57 LIFESTYLE
City life • Education • Welfare • Tribal and village life • The family and marriage • Secret societies

71 RELIGION
Tribal religions • Totemism • Magic • Christianity • Indigenous African Christianity • Islam

CONTENTS

79 LANGUAGE
English • Regional languages • Lingua francas • Written languages • Other influences

87 ARTS
Literature • Americo-Liberian literature • Folktales • Architecture • Music • A living art and craft

97 LEISURE
Leisure in the cities • Rural leisure activities • Leisure for expatriates • Sports • The media • Games and songs

105 FESTIVALS
Christian festivals • Muslim festivals • African festivals • The Woi epic • Weddings • Secret society festivals • Birth rituals • Funeral celebration

113 FOOD
Staples • Meat • Other foods • A typical meal • A Liberian feast • Eating out • Beverages • Kitchen equipment

122 MAP OF LIBERIA

124 QUICK NOTES

125 GLOSSARY

126 BIBLIOGRAPHY

126 INDEX

The Liberation Monument in Monrovia.

GEOGRAPHY

LIBERIA IS LOCATED IN West Africa, a few degrees north of the equator. It is bordered by Sierra Leone in the northwest, Guinea in the north, the Ivory Coast in the east, and the Atlantic Ocean in the south and west.

Nearly all of the country is made up of Precambrian rocks, Earth's oldest rocks. The Precambrian era began with the formation of Earth some 4.6 billion years ago and ended around 590 million years ago. Liberia's metamorphic rocks (gneiss and schist) and igneous rock (granite) form the West African Shield, the name geologists give to a rock formation about 3 billion years old.

The form of the land falls into three main regions: coastal lowlands, plateaus, and highlands. Most of the land inland from the coastal strip is covered by tropical rainforest. Although it is threatened by deforestation, Liberia's rainforest remains the largest in West Africa.

The first national census, taken in 1962, recorded a population of one million. The last census, in 1990, showed a population of 2.5 million. Even though the present estimate is over 3 million, this does not indicate a very high population density given the size of the country.

In the past, the relatively small population slowed economic growth. In the late 1950s, for example, when diamond mines were producing a rich yield, the government closed down some of the mines because the increased need for miners was drawing labor from coffee plantations and iron ore mines. This is no longer a serious problem. The main center of population is around the capital city of Monrovia.

Above: Liberia's rainforest is the largest expanse of rainforest in West Africa.

Opposite: The low and sandy coastline extends for 370 miles (595 km). From the sea it appears remarkably flat, with only a few hills rising above 50 feet (15 m).

7

The St. John is one of several rivers running parallel to one another, flowing from the north toward the Atlantic Ocean.

RIVERS

Some of Liberia's rivers help form the country's national boundaries. The Mano rises in the Guinea Highlands and forms 90 miles (145 km) of the border with Sierra Leone. In the east, the Cavalla originates north of the Nimba Mountains in Guinea and flows south, forming the border with the Ivory Coast. The St. Paul marks Liberia's border with Guinea for part of its journey. One important river that traverses the entire width of the country, the Lofa, has its origin in Guinea.

Like the Lofa, several other major rivers flow more or less parallel with one another from the north toward the sea. The 125 mile (200 km) St. Paul is the most important, reaching the Atlantic fairly close to the port at Monrovia. The river is an important source of water to agricultural land in the interior, but it is not a convenient source of transportation to and from the capital's port. This is because the St. Paul, like most of the country's rivers, has several rapids and waterfalls inland, where the gradient of the river is steep, with rocky stretches closer to the coast, making navigation difficult in places. In addition, seasonal rainfall followed by rapid runoff from the rivers causes sudden changes in water levels. The St. Paul is navigable for 18 miles (30 km) upstream from the coast, while the Cavalla can be navigated for 50 miles (80 km) from its mouth in the Gulf of Guinea.

The force of the rivers has, however, been exploited to generate hydroelectric power. There are hydroelectric plants on St. Paul and on Farmington River, a tributary of the Lofa.

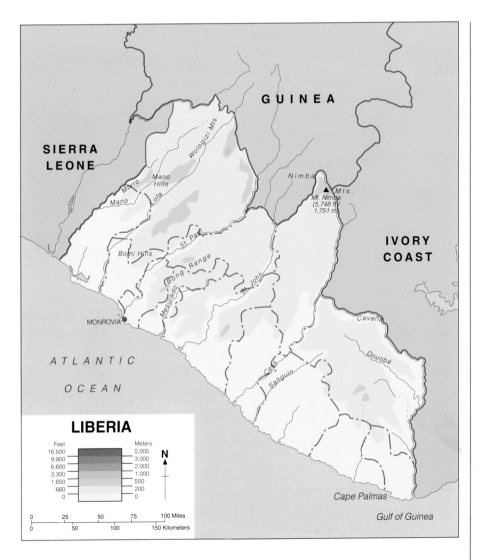

LIBERIA

Feet	Meters
16,500	5,000
9,900	3,000
6,600	2,000
3,300	1,000
1,650	500
660	200
0	0

N

0   25   50   75   100 Miles
0   50   100   150 Kilometers

COASTAL LOWLANDS

Liberia's coastline, 10 to 25 miles (16–40 km) wide, has many estuaries formed by rivers rising in the north. Wave action has caused long sandbars to form in front of the shallow lagoons and mangrove marshes of the coast. The sandbars keep shifting, and this, plus the rocky nature of many of the rivers draining into the sea, means there are no natural harbors. Since the coastline is fertile, settlements have grown up along it. The largest cities— Monrovia, Marshall, and Buchanan—are on the coast.

HILLS AND PLATEAUS

Plateaus are areas of high and level ground, and in Liberia they gradually rise from a series of rolling hills with foothills close to the coast. The hills were the first places to be mined for iron ore and were once far more important to the country's economy than they are now. The plateaus have an average height of just under 1,000 feet (305 m), though those farthest inland rise above 1,500 feet (457 m).

Some parts of the plateaus remain relatively unexplored because of dense, impenetrable rainforests and rivers that are not easily navigated. Parts of the hilly country, on the other hand, are home to many of the country's biggest coffee plantations.

The highlands rise to about 4,000 feet (1,220 m) above sea level and continue across all three of Liberia's borders. In the northeast they cross

Above: **A dirt road runs by a village near Mt. Nimba. Villages in this region are few and far between.**

Below: **The Nimba Mountains are located where the borders of Liberia, the Ivory Coast, and Guinea meet.**

A coffee tree with beans and flowers. Some of the country's largest coffee plantations are in the hills.

over into Guinea, where they form the foothills of the Guinea Highlands, while farther east they include the Nimba Mountains and cross over into the Ivory Coast and Guinea. Mt. Nimba at Guest House Hill (5,748 ft/ 1,751 m)—the highest peak in Liberia—is located here, close to the point where the borders of the Ivory Coast, Guinea, and Liberia meet. At the western end of these highlands are the Wologizi Mountains, close to Sierra Leone. Not surprisingly, the mountainous regions of the highlands are the least developed and least populated parts of the country.

GEOGRAPHY STATISTICS

Total area: 43,000 square miles (111,370 sq km)—a little smaller than the state of Mississippi

Coastline: 370 miles (595 km)

Land boundaries: 985 miles (1,585 km)—shared with Guinea for 350 miles (563 km), the Ivory Coast for 445 miles (716 km), and Sierra Leone for 190 miles (306 km)

Moderate temperatures and high humidity ensure lush vegetation in Liberia all year round.

CLIMATE

Daily temperatures in Liberia range from 26°C to 32°C (79°F to 90°F), which combined with a relative humidity that averages 88%, make most days extremely hot and sticky. Although there is a rainy season, rainfall is irregular. The rainy season begins earlier on the coast than it does in the interior. Between May and November is the wet season, when relative humidity reaches as high as 95%, but usually around July or August there is a brief period that resembles the dry season of December to April.

One of the few respites from the high humidity of this equatorial climate comes toward the end of the year when the dust-laden desert winds known as the harmattan blow from the Sahara region toward western Liberia. The dry season has been lengthened by almost a month in recent years, due to deforestation and drought in the Sahel—a vast semidesert region north of Liberia.

The heaviest rainfall is along the coast, since that is where the rainy season begins earliest, and Cape Mount records as much as 205 inches (5,200 mm) every year. The northwest coastal region receives a fairly high amount, recording 160 inches (4,000 mm) annually, while the southeast coastal region receives an average of about 100 inches (2,500 mm). In the interior the average annual rainfall is about half that of coastal regions.

The relative humidity is also lower away from the coast. During the dry season days are still hot but not unpleasantly so, and nights are comfortably cool. Across the country, rainfall takes the characteristic form of long and heavy downpours that may last from a few hours or up to two or three days.

MONROVIA

The capital city, Monrovia, is situated on the coast and is spread across an area divided by lagoons into a number of small islands. Monrovia was founded in 1822 on the left bank of the St. Paul River on the ridge formed by Cape Mesurado. Because it is situated at a height, it offers a panoramic view of the Atlantic Ocean and the coastal plains. Monrovia and its suburbs occupy five square miles (13 sq. km). The layout of the city, which follows a neat grid pattern, is testimony to the North American origins of the first settlers who designed Monrovia. Some old buildings are reminiscent of the old architecture of the southern United States.

The main port and center of industrial activity is on Bushrod Island, which benefits from a deepwater harbor that was constructed with the help of US aid between 1944 and 1948. Apart from a main wharf where large ships can load and unload, there are specially built piers for the shipping of iron ore. In addition there is an oil jetty, and Roberts International Airport is nearby.

The population of Monrovia represents all of the country's ethnic groups, as well as refugees, other Africans, Lebanese and other Asians, and Europeans.

The leopard is mainly nocturnal, but it sometimes basks in the sun.

WILDLIFE

Liberia has over 100 species of mammals that include various members of the cat family. The leopard, one of the smaller big cats, is the largest cat found there. It can grow to 6 feet 6 inches (2 m) in length, including the tail. Its prey includes monkeys. The number of leopards in Liberia, as elsewhere, is decreasing, but there is no shortage of monkeys in the country. These share the rainforest with animals such as the chimpanzee, antelope, pygmy hippopotamus, elephant, and anteater. Also found in the rainforest are scorpions, lizards, at least eight varieties of poisonous snakes, and many unusual birds and bats. Three types of crocodile live along the banks of the rivers.

Two of the rarer mammals found in Liberia are the manatee and the pygmy hippopotamus. Manatees are aquatic herbivorous mammals, which have been overhunted for their meat. The West African species of manatee, *Trichebus sengalensis,* is far less common than it once was. Hippopotamuses are some of the largest land mammals, but the pygmy

Chimpanzees abound in the Liberian forests.

hippopotamus, *Choerpsis liberiensis*, is a modest 3 feet (90 cm) tall and is found in the wild only in West Africa. Its black back has a greenish sheen that provides it with a camouflage in its habitat of coastal forests, rivers, and marshland. The larger species of hippopotamus spends far more time in the water and is more likely to travel in herds than its Liberian relation, but they both feed on grasses and reeds and travel many miles along the river at night.

The rainforest environment and the coastal habitat supports a rich diversity of bird life. Parrots, hornbills, and woodpeckers are common in the forests, and along the coast flamingoes search for small animals and algae in the muddy waters of the lagoons. The flamingo uses its crooked bill to filter its food from the brackish water.

The political instability that has plagued Liberia in recent years has resulted in poor control over poaching, and this has contributed to the number of animal species now facing extinction. Elephants, bush cows, and leopards are slowly but steadily disappearing from Liberia.

The rarest animal found in Liberia is the Liberian mongoose (Liberiictis kuhni), which was thought to be extinct until a live male was captured in 1989. Even if a female is found, the species will remain highly endangered.

PLANT LIFE

The rubber tree is one of the most important trees in Liberia because of its economic value. The average rubber tree grows to about 81 feet (25 m) and yields a milky white fluid called latex, from which rubber is produced. Early in the 20th century a British-German company began producing rubber for export from wild rubber trees in Liberia, and it was not long before a plantation was created and thousands of rubber trees planted. The first plantation was forced to close down after some years because of falling world rubber prices, but when the market improved in the mid-1920s, the Firestone Tire and Rubber Company acquired the plantation and expanded it to about 1 million acres (405,000 hectares).

Latex is collected by cutting into the bark of the rubber tree and collecting the flow in a small cup. Each cut yields only a tablespoonful of latex, but a new cut can be made every other day. The trees are periodically left to renew themselves.

The latex is collected from a rubber tree in a small cup. When a sufficient amount of latex has been collected it is mixed with water, and acid is added to help the particles of rubber adhere to one another. This allows the rubber to be compressed by a machine, and the sheets of rubber that emerge from the machine's rollers are then dried.

Another economically important tree is the coffee tree, more than one species of which flourishes in Liberia. Until Brazil began to dominate the market in the late 19th century, Liberia's economy was bolstered by the export of coffee from the indigenous species *coffea liberica*. This species is still cultivated in the coastal region, but it produces an inferior type of coffee that has a bitter taste. In the north of the country the imported species, *coffea robusta*, which is largely used in the manufacture of instant coffee, is far more common.

The kola tree, native to tropical Africa, is also found in Liberia. It is popular for its nuts, which provide a source of caffeine when chewed. There is a small export trade of kola nuts to Guinea.

HISTORY

VERY LITTLE IS KNOWN about the people who inhabited the land that became Liberia in the early 19th century. The country is Africa's oldest independent republic and dates back to 1822, when US philanthropic organizations succeeded in establishing an African home for former slaves. They were partly inspired by Britain's effort in settling former slaves in Sierra Leone, but an attempt to do the same with former US slaves slowed down after the death of Paul Cuffee, who originated the project.

In 1816 the United States began negotiations with local rulers over the possibility of acquiring sufficient land to form a settlement for freed slaves. The following year the American Colonization Society was founded with the intention of resettling emancipated slaves and freeborn Africans, and by 1821 the society was able to purchase the area around Cape Mesurado, later renaming the settlement Monrovia. Within a year the first people arrived from the United States, and in 1824 the name Liberia was adopted.

Initially, a majority of emancipated slaves in the United States opposed the "back to Africa" idea and argued that the United States was their country because their hard labor had helped create it.

Opposite: **The Memorial to Independence in Monrovia.**

Left: **Monrovia in the 1880s.**

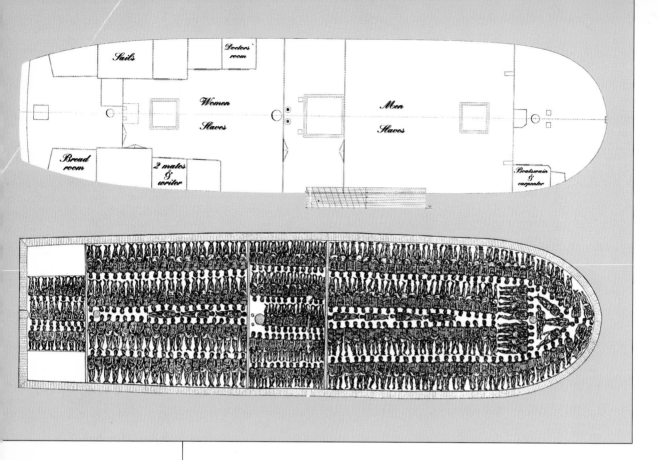

The slaves who were transported to the plantations of the European colonies in the Americas had to endure severe hardships along the way. They were crowded into the lower decks of the slave ships so that they barely had room to move.

EARLY HISTORY

When the Sahara region began to dry up, around 2000 B.C., some of its inhabitants are believed to have moved south and penetrated into West Africa. Liberia's first inhabitants were probably the descendants of these people. It is also thought that Mande-speaking tribes migrated to Liberia from regions now belonging to Ghana and Mali. Kru tribes are thought to have been among the earliest of these arrivals, coming sometime after A.D. 1000.

After A.D. 1400, waves of immigration saw new tribal groups moving into Liberia—the Krahn, Grebo, Gio (also known as Dan), and Mandingo from the Ivory Coast, the Mano from Ghana, and the Vai from Sierra Leone. The Bassa, Dei, Kpelle, and Kissi also arrived around this time. The reasons for these population shifts are not fully known, but the conquest and decline of the ancient empire of Ghana (in modern Mali and Mauritania) may have led some groups to flee south to escape their Muslim conquerors. These groups are significant because they brought with them the skills of iron smelting, cloth weaving, and cotton spinning, as well as important new crops such as rice.

The identity of the first Europeans to reach Liberia has not been established. Hanno, a Carthaginian navigator in the fifth century B.C., made an exploratory voyage down the west coast of Africa, but French traders in the 14th and early 15th centuries are thought to have been the first to trade with the Africans living there. In 1461 a Portuguese mariner, Pedro de Sintra, reached the coast of Liberia and paved the way for later Portuguese explorers, who largely restricted themselves to mapping the coastline since the inland rainforest presented a formidable natural barrier. Early traders were interested in the Liberian coast because that was where they collected melegueta pepper. Years later, for the British and French, the slave trade proved to be the motivating factor.

Numerically, the entire present population of Liberia, around 3 million, represents less than a third of all those Africans who were transported to the New World from their homelands in West Africa.

GRAINS OF PARADISE

The Africans in what is now Liberia first made contact with Portuguese traders because of the latter's need to add flavor to the dull food they stored dry for consumption in the winter months. *Aframomum melegueta* (melegueta pepper), a plant belonging to the ginger family and native to parts of West Africa, bore seeds that were used as a spice and a medicine. They were so highly valued that they were known as "grains of paradise," and in time part of the coastal area of Liberia became known as the Grain Coast. Christopher Columbus sailed to Sierra Leone for the Portuguese and very likely traded for pepper along the Grain Coast.

The Liberian flag has eleven equal stripes of red alternating with white. A blue square in the top corner on the side that is hoisted contains a white five-pointed star.

FOUNDING A COUNTRY

In 1794 the United States declared the slave trade illegal, and in the early 19th century the Grain Coast was suggested as a possible home for freed slaves. In 1818, less than 30 years after abolition, two US government officials journeyed across the Atlantic with representatives from the American Colonization Society, and together they held discussions with African tribal chiefs. These talks were at first unsuccessful, but in 1821 an agreement was signed between the society and the African king Peter, allowing the society to become the owner of land. The following year the society and six other like-minded philanthropic organizations supervised the first repatriation of freed black slaves to Africa. At this stage the territory in question was a relatively small area in the vicinity of what is now Monrovia.

A white American who played an influential part in Liberia's early history as a nation was Jehudi Ashmun (1794–1828). At the age of 24 he wrote a report for the American Colonization Society that called for renewed efforts to continue the work of Paul Cuffee. He arrived in Liberia in 1822 and remained there until his death in 1828. He set about adding new territory to the colony, and within three years he had negotiated a new treaty with local tribal chiefs. He also helped establish a system of government and encouraged the development of a rudimentary form of commerce. At the same time other settlements were being founded along the coast by other philanthropic organizations; the towns of Greenville and Harper were established in this way.

In 1839 the first governor, Thomas Buchanan, was appointed. When he died two years later he was replaced by an African, Joseph Jenkins Roberts, who had been born free in Virginia. Under Roberts the territory expanded, and in 1847 Liberia announced its independence from the American Colonization Society. In 1857 a separate colony that had also been founded by one of the philanthropic groups, christened "Maryland in Liberia" and with its capital at Harper, joined the new state of Liberia.

There remained some disagreement with the colonial powers of Britain and France over the demarcation of the new country's borders, because these two countries had vested interests in the states neighboring Liberia. By 1919, however, the last of these differences, with France, were ironed out. The exact boundaries that were agreed on at that time are the ones that continue to define Liberian territory to this day.

The 1821 sale of land by the African king Peter was "agreed upon" after the American Robert Stockton held a pistol to the king's head.

PAUL CUFFEE

Paul Cuffee (1759–1817), a rich Quaker of African-American and Native American descent, made his fortune in shipping. He was one of the first to support the concept of financing former slaves who wanted to leave the United States and settle in Africa. His idea was to make one trip every year with settlers and cover the costs by bringing back African produce for sale in the United States. In 1816 he carried through his plan and landed in Freetown, Sierra Leone, with nearly 40 former slaves on his ship, *Elizabeth*. He died the following year, however, and while his plans seemed to have died with him, he had succeeded in convincing people of the viability of his project. Groups such as the American Colonization Society took up his dream and made it a reality.

The Danish steamer *Horsa* left Savannah, Georgia, on March 19, 1895, with 200 freed slaves bound for Liberia.

MONEY PROBLEMS

Until the declaration of independence in 1847, Liberia received cash subsidies from the colonization societies that had been involved in the country's establishment. This could not continue indefinitely, and when the aid stopped, the country faced financial ruin. For the next 80 years Liberia turned to European nations for assistance. Britain provided a large loan in 1871, and a British-German company established the first rubber plantation in 1906.

A lack of capital investment and money compounded the problems that faced the first settlers. Without adequate provision for training in new skills, the former slaves were left to their own resources. For many of them, the challenge of adopting a rural African lifestyle and abandoning the US culture they had been brought up in proved very difficult. What made matters worse was that the indigenous African inhabitants did not readily accept the new arrivals. Many of the latter gave up trying to make a living from agriculture and turned to trade in coffee, sugar, palm oil, and cocoa.

One result of these difficulties was a national debt that increased every year. The relatively healthy trade in the export of coffee to northern Europe suffered a setback in the years after Liberian coffee was introduced into Brazil; the South American country eventually came to dominate the world market. The 1870s witnessed a fall in world prices for cocoa and sugar, and this helped bring on an economic crisis that plagued Liberia for nearly the next 60 years.

NATIONAL RECOVERY

In 1926 Firestone established its rubber plantation near Monrovia. It was the largest rubber plantation in the world and remained the country's biggest employer for the next 45 years. Liberia benefited by being granted an annual revenue from the company, and a large loan secured through the company went toward settling outstanding national debts.

A new problem arose shortly after, when it was alleged that Liberia was involved in sending Africans as virtual slaves to Spanish plantations in Spanish Guinea. The president resigned over the issue, and a new administration was formed under President Edwin Barclay in 1930. Further financial difficulties led to the League of Nations—a forerunner to the United Nations—offering a new assistance package, which was eventually accepted in new discussions with Firestone.

In the 1920s, at a time when 90% of the country's trade was with Europe and only 5% with the United States, help came from an unlikely source— the Firestone Tire and Rubber Company of the United States.

Latex is carried in buckets to the processing plant at the Firestone plantation. Firestone established the largest rubber plantation in the world near Monrovia.

The United States helped in the construction of a deepwater harbor at Bushrod Island.

WORLD WAR II

Liberia was affected significantly by World War II, though not in the way most countries were. There was no military involvement by Liberia, and it was not until January 1944, after the election of William V.S. Tubman as president, that the country officially declared war on Japan and Germany.

In 1942, however, Liberia and the United States signed a defense agreement that changed Liberia's previously insignificant role on the world political stage to one of prominence. This was because the Japanese invasion and occupation of Southeast Asia denied the West its source of rubber. Apart from Ceylon (modern Sri Lanka), the only remaining source of natural rubber open to the United States and its allies was the Firestone plantation in Liberia, and rubber was urgently needed for the war effort.

The terms of the defense agreement resulted in the United States investing in the development of Liberia's transportation infrastructure. Roads were built, and an international airport and deepwater harbor were constructed in Monrovia.

Confirmation of the growing involvement of the United States in Liberian affairs came when the US dollar replaced the former British-backed currency as legal tender. Liberia's signing of the United Nations declaration in 1944—it was one of only four African nations to sign— symbolized its emergence as a fully fledged independent nation, although one that was closely tied to the United States.

PEACE BEFORE THE STORM

In 1960 Liberia took its seat in the United Nations, and when the Organization of African Unity (OAU) was formed three years later, Liberia was one of the four founding member states.

From 1944 to 1971 Tubman was the country's president. When he died in office, his vice-president assumed the presidency. William Tolbert, the new president, faced economic problems arising from a fall in world prices of rubber and iron ore, but on the world stage Liberia was heralded as a stable African nation uniquely able to effect a peaceful and constitutional transfer of power. Most other parts of Africa were experiencing turbulent times.

When the government increased the price of rice in 1980, a number of anti-government demonstrations took place and leaders of an opposition party were imprisoned when they called for a general strike. Within a month, Tolbert was killed in an army coup and Liberia's hope for stability was rudely shattered. The new leader was Samuel Doe, whose army rank was that of master sergeant when he assumed power at the head of a new People's Redemption Council. Part of the reason for the violent overthrow of Tolbert's government was that the Americo-Liberians, people descended from the former slaves who came to Liberia in the 19th century, dominated political power. The majority of Liberians belonged to the various indigenous tribes that had long lived in this part of West Africa, and they had become increasingly disappointed with governments that were dominated by Americo-Liberians.

A guard at the Executive Mansion in Monrovia presents arms. The April 1980 revolution, which brought Samuel Doe to power, was launched amid a spate of bloody executions.

The disabled victim of a mine attack walks past a poster hailing the end of the fighting.

Half a million Liberians became refugees in neighboring countries as the country drew closer to civil war in 1990.

CIVIL WAR

The People's Redemption Council claimed to be uniting the country, but the constitution was suspended and political parties were banned. In 1985 elections were held, but it is generally agreed that the results were rigged to ensure the election of Doe as president. He formally took over in 1986.

In 1989 a rebel army based in Sierra Leone and led by Charles Taylor crossed into Liberia. A bitter struggle followed between various ethnic factions—Doe was largely supported by the Krahn and Mandingo, while Taylor's army was mostly Gio and Mano. Some order was restored when the Economic Community of West African States (ECOWAS) organized a peacekeeping force. Taylor retaliated by establishing his own capital in Gbarnga and proclaiming himself president. Doe was killed by a group belonging to another rebel leader, Prince Johnson.

PEACE AT LAST?

The civil war dragged on, with no one side able to achieve a decisive military advantage or come to a lasting agreement with its political opponents. In 1993 the United Nations negotiated a treaty between the main factions, but the provisional government failed to carry through the terms of the treaty. In 1995 there was another attempt at a truce, and the armed factions agreed to a peace deal.

The civil war seems to have finally ended, with the signing of the Abuja Accord in 1996. The estimated 30,000 to 60,000 fighters have given up their weapons and are no longer seen carrying arms, although caches of weapons continue to be discovered. On July 19, 1997, in a vote judged fair by international observers, Charles Taylor was elected president of Liberia. Since his election there has been no further violence.

Refugees return from Guinea to their devastated homeland.

The OAU, which was founded with the help of Liberia, was formed with an anti-colonial agenda and with the intention of confirming the territorial integrity of African states.

29

GOVERNMENT

THE HISTORY OF GOVERNMENT in Liberia points to the problems that eventually tore the country apart as well as shows what was achieved. The earliest constitution followed the example of the United States but denied the majority of the population many of the constitutional rights that should have been extended to them. The indigenous tribes were not treated as equals, and a political elite developed out of the early America-Liberians and their descendants. Under the presidency of Tubman some attempts were made to deal with this by extending the vote to all adults, including women, who paid taxes and owned property. This was not universal suffrage, and although it was a step forward it made little difference to most Liberians.

Government under the presidency of Tolbert underwent a more progressive change. Universal suffrage was introduced, and the constitution was amended so that no president could stand for reelection. It turned out to be too little too late, and the military takeover launched by Doe was supported by those who thought a new and fairer system of government would emerge. A new constitution was drawn up in 1986, but it was not very different from the preceding one, and controversy over Doe's election as president robbed it of much of its legitimacy. Beginning in 1990, a civil war raged across the country for nearly seven years with no one group able to govern the whole country. The peace treaty that was signed in mid-1995 put government in the hands of a new Council of State. The Council of State was dissolved in 1997, after Taylor was elected president of the country.

Above: **The Ministry of Public Labor building in Monrovia.**

Opposite: **William Tubman Monument in Monrovia. Tubman, a lawyer by profession, worked as a county attorney, judge, and preacher before becoming president.**

31

THE TRUE WHIGS

From 1878 until the coup in 1980, political power was in the hands of the True Whig Party. No other political party in the world has managed to remain in power uninterrupted for so long. The party was named after a British political party called the Whigs, which dominated the politics of its country in the 18th century.

The True Whig Party was the preserve of the Americo-Liberians, and it was through this party that the latter retained control of the National Assembly. It was the only organized political party in Liberia for many years, but it maintained the appearance of needing popular support by a series of nomination conventions for the National Assembly, at which "candidates" were "elected"—although most of the decisions were made in smoke-filled rooms long before the conventions took place. There were no limits on the sums that local businessmen could give to the party, and civil servants had "contributions to the party" deducted from their salaries.

The National Assembly had a Senate and a House of Representatives, but over time the two chambers became little more than debating clubs because the True Whigs always had a majority and the president was always a member of the same party.

THE COUNCIL OF STATE

Until recently Liberia was governed by a six-member Council of State under a chairperson who was politically neutral. This was part of the peace deal signed by the warring factions in 1995. The last chair of the council was Ruth Perry. Her appointment in 1996 made her the first female head of an African state.

The council consisted of representatives of the various factions that fought one another in the civil war, as well as two civilian members. One of the most important groups was the National Patriotic Front of Liberia (NPFL) under the leadership of Taylor. The NPFL disarmed in 1996, and in early 1997 it became the National Patriotic Party (NPP), a civilian group. On August 2, two weeks after Taylor was elected president of Liberia, the Council of State was dissolved.

Liberia's first government was modeled on the United States system. It has a red, white, and blue flag and a capital named after a US president.

Opposite: **The Executive Mansion in Monrovia, where the president lives. In March 1990 President Doe made a speech on its balcony, appealing to Nigeria to help quell the uprising led by Charles Taylor.**

Left: **Supporters of Charles Taylor waved branches to greet their candidate during a campaign rally in Gbarnga.**

TWENTIETH-CENTURY HEADS OF GOVERNMENT

President

1900–04:   Garretson Wilmot Gibson
1904–12:   Arthur Barclay
1912–20:   Daniel Edward Howard
1920–30:   Charles Dunbar King
1930–43:   Edwin Barclay
1943–71:   William Tubman
1971–80:   William Richard Tolbert

Chairman of People's Redemption Council

1980–86:   Samuel K. Doe

President

1986–90:   Samuel K. Doe
1990–96:   A state of civil war with different regions of the country controlled by various armed factional groups
1997–   Charles Taylor

Chair of Council of State

1995–96:   Wilton G.S. Sankawulo
1996–97:   Ruth Perry

Left: **Samuel Doe.**

Right: **William Richard Tolbert.**

Opposite: **A Dan chief. Tribal chiefs are important links between the governments at the center and in the villages.**

LOCAL GOVERNMENT

Local government for most of the country is based around 13 counties: Bomi, Bong, Grand Bassa, Grand Cape Mount, Grand Gedeh, Grand Kru, Lofa, Margibi, Maryland, Montserrado, Nimba, Rivercess, and Sino. Every county has one administrative official who is appointed by the central government, and there is no elected local council. Monrovia is governed directly by the government, and there are also two territories that, like the counties, are broken down into various districts. The districts are subdivided into a number of smaller administrative regions, each of which comes under the rule of a tribal chief.

The tribal chiefs are important links between the central and local governments. One of the chiefs' responsibilities is the functioning of the tribal courts, where local disputes are aired and misdemeanors dealt with.

HUMAN PAWNS

In parts of Liberia local government continues to be dominated by members of small but powerful families. Behind the power lies wealth, and in this sense little has changed over the centuries, but in the past wealth was acquired and maintained by a process of owning people that was close to a state of domestic slavery. It was known as pawning and occurred when someone exchanged either themselves or one of their children for a sum of money or valuable possessions, such as farm animals. In return, the person who was pawned was committed to working for the lender until the debt was paid. A clan leader or tribal chief could demonstrate his wealth and influence by building a large pool of pawns.

A Dan chief, the staff of authority on his shoulder, stands in front of his house specially decorated with wall painting.

LOCAL CHIEFS

Tribal chiefs continue to play an important role in local government in Liberia. Until the troubles in the 1980s and civil war in the 1990s most Liberians outside of the capital had experienced government only in the form of village meetings under a tribal chief. A recent development has been the establishment of paramount chiefs who govern a far larger area than before.

Historically, the choice of an individual as a local chief was often made from a small number of influential families, or clans, and tremendous social prestige is still associated with the role of tribal chief. To some extent age is a factor, with the most elderly members of a prestigious family having a strong claim to leadership. A significant exception to this pattern developed among some of the tribes in the northwest of the country. This region had a relatively unstable past, and opportunities arose for adventurous groups to achieve tribal power rather than simply being born into it. There was a tradition of slave trading that allowed successful individuals to emerge as leaders who could maintain their position through acquired wealth and force of arms.

One of the duties of tribal chiefs is to mediate in disputes between villagers. Often disputes are caused by the breakup of a marriage, when the two families are eager to divide the couple's goods to their own advantage. The husband's family wants their bride price back, while the wife seeks to keep it as compensation for her years of work. It is the chief's job to keep all sides happy, since they must all live as neighbors afterward.

SYSTEMS OF JUSTICE

A system of criminal law based on a Western model, with judges, juries, and courts of law, has always existed in Liberia. The Supreme Court is headed by a chief justice, who is helped by five associate justices. The latter are all appointed by the president. However, the Western system of law has functioned effectively only in the area around the capital and in large towns.

The civil war saw the collapse of the criminal law system as power passed into the hands of rival groups who established their own summary forms of justice. A major challenge facing the country as it tries to rebuild itself is to reassert a system of justice that goes beyond the imprisonment and execution of political rivals.

In rural areas more traditional methods of tribal law have operated, through chiefs and village communities of elders. The traditional forms of justice that exist in these areas depend for their success on the respect that is accorded to tribal chiefs and village elders. The legal precepts are not the result of government legislation, and law books are not consulted when considering a case.

One traditional form of justice no longer practiced is trial by ordeal. In this custom a person accused of a serious crime would have to go through some painful ordeal as a test of integrity and honesty, for example, drinking a poison made from the bark of the sasswood tree. The theory, apparently, was that a guilty person would find it difficult to maintain the bluff of innocence when faced with the possibility of death by poison.

The Temple of Justice in Monrovia. The Western system of law has functioned effectively in the capital and major towns except during the civil war.

37

ECONOMY

THE MAINSTAY OF LIBERIA'S market economy is agriculture, with 7 out of 10 Liberians earning their living on the land. More women than men are engaged in agriculture, although men make up 60% of the country's labor force. Others are employed mainly in manufacturing concerns and various types of administration and service. There are no state-owned industries.

One consequence of the country's dependence on agriculture is that consumer goods and raw materials have to be imported on a large scale. The cost of this is somewhat balanced by exports from the mining, forestry, and rubber industries. Other important exports are cacao, coffee, and palm kernels. Diamonds are also exported. Most exports go to the European Union—especially Germany, Italy, and France—and the United States. The chief imports are machinery, metals, textiles, and foodstuffs, mostly from the United States and Germany. Liberia has accumulated an external debt of over two billion US dollars and it is believed to be rising.

The US dollar used to be legal tender in Liberia, and although this is no longer the case, the Liberian dollar's official value keeps parity with the US dollar. Unofficially, the Liberian dollar is worth a lot less than its US counterpart.

Opposite: **Liberia's economy is based on agriculture. A woman displays a canful of grain she is selling at the market in Bong Mines.**

Left: **A rubber plantation near Monrovia. Despite the importance of rubber to Liberia's economy, the country accounts for less than 5% of world production.**

A child in Monrovia scrambles over a rotting mass of garbage in search of something to sell. The capital is still recovering from the war, when its infrastructure was heavily damaged.

THE LEGACY OF WAR

The civil war of the 1990s has done more to weaken Liberia's economy than any other factor, and its long-term effects will continue into the next century. The constant fighting damaged the country's infrastructure, including its roads, bridges, and ports, and because the area around the capital was the center of the political struggle, this was where the maximum damage occurred. Unfortunately, the area around Monrovia is home to much of the country's industry—a petroleum refinery, cement plants, and factories—and this type of industrial activity has suffered considerably from the weakened infrastructure.

The fighting also eroded people's confidence in the country's economic future and led to a serious lack of investment both at home and from abroad. Businesspeople, like many other citizens, fled the country, taking with them their skills and capital. Nearly all foreign nationals, many of them engaged in commercial business, also left. The civil unrest severely dented the tourist trade, and although the latter was never a major economic asset, the war prevented its potential from being developed.

In the long term, the most damaging consequence of the war was its effect on the country's education system. Because of the economy's reliance on agriculture, governments before the outbreak of the civil war had been developing vocational education programs. Young Liberians were being trained to earn a living in commerce and industry—but the collapse of centralized government brought all such national programs to a halt.

NATURAL RESOURCES

Liberia's most important natural resource is iron ore. Other natural resources include gold, diamonds, lead, graphite, and manganese, and there have also been finds of bauxite, copper, tin, zinc, and barite. In the early 1980s deposits of uranium were identified in the counties of Bong and Lofa.

It is widely believed that there are reserves of oil off the Atlantic coast. Potential oil fields are in the process of being mapped, through agreements with foreign oil companies, but it may be some time before the country is able to exploit this resource. One resource that is being exploited, though not to its full capacity, is water for generating electricity. Almost half the electric power used in the country now comes from hydroelectricity. The largest generating station is on the St. Paul River, not far from Monrovia.

The sea is also a natural resource, providing a source of mackerel and barracuda, and there are a number of Liberian fishing companies. In recent years, several inland fishing concerns using artificial ponds to breed fish have been established.

The Lamco mines, along with other iron mines, make Liberia one of the leading exporters of iron ore in Africa.

The tropical rainforest is a valuable source of hardwood timber, and the government operates a system of concessions that give companies—not always Liberian—the right to exploit a predetermined area of forest in return for a fee. It was not until the 1970s, however, that the first reforestation programs began, and a substantial proportion of the country's natural forests has been depleted.

FARMING

There are some large farms that are operated as commercial businesses. The owners are often foreign companies, but the managers who run the farms on a day-to-day basis are Liberians. Most farms, though, are small and belong to a family. Though these farms are individually small, their total value to the country's economy is equal to that of the large ones.

A typical small farmer cultivates rice, cassava, and vegetables, and keeps animals such as goats and chickens. The animals have a cash value as well as provide an important source of food for the family's own needs. Farmers also earn cash by cultivating coffee, cacao, oil palms, and sugarcane. Many farmers are members of local cooperatives, and they sell their cash crops to their cooperative, which in turn sells them in bulk to merchants.

Projects have been launched to raise rice production, and international aid programs have helped in this endeavor.

The cultivation of rice makes an essential contribution to the feeding of the country's population, but because the yield is low a significant quantity also needs to be imported every year.

As mentioned earlier, in 1926 a US company, Firestone, acquired the first rubber plantation in Liberia and expanded it on a large scale. It also established other plantations. It had around 10,000 employees at its two plantations in Harbel and Cavalla, and in 1983 it sold its Cavalla plantation to another company. Although Firestone is still one of the largest employers in the country, a number of other American and European companies have now established their own smaller plantations. There are also many independent rubber farmers who plant their own rubber trees, and sell the latex to foreign firms that handle the refining process.

Food accounts for about one-third of Liberia's total imports.

DOMESTIC ECONOMY: THE COCONUT PALM

A vital component of the village economy is the coconut palm. Its branches are used in house building and thatching. String and raffia are made from the stripped leaves, and from these the villagers make baskets, nets, and even clothes. The fruit is used to make cooking oil, which is the base of palm butter soup. It is also made into candles, soap, cosmetics, and, of course, palm wine. The inner nuts are dried to make nut meat that can be stored or sold, while the shells are burned to make ash for soap. Kitchen utensils, brooms, and fences also come from the palm tree.

TRANSPORTATION

Liberia's underdevelopment is related to the fact that an estimated three-quarters of the country's roads are not passable year-round. The problem was compounded by the civil war, when roads were badly damaged and there was no investment in road building or maintenance. The result is that the country presently has only two reliable routes that can be used by trucks transporting heavy goods. Both highways lead to Monrovia, one from Buchanan and the other from Kakata. There is a vital railroad link, with a total of over 300 miles (480 km) of track, that connects the port with the areas where iron ore is mined. The railway was built by the mining companies, which still own and operate the lines for the transportation of iron ore to the port. There are many small airstrips in the interior, while the international airport, built by the United States during World War II, is situated to the east of the capital.

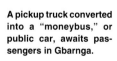

A pickup truck converted into a "moneybus," or public car, awaits passengers in Gbarnga.

With Monrovia being a free port, it is common to see large oceangoing vessels around the world displaying Liberia as their country of registration. There are over 1,600 ships from various nations carrying Liberian registration, which means the country can lay claim to one of the largest tanker fleets in the world. Even though Liberia does not own these ships, the country earns valuable foreign currency from the annual fees it is able to charge.

Monrovia is the only free port in West Africa: foreign goods can be stored and redistributed to other ships without the payment of duty.

IRON ORE

In the 1960s the production of rubber, until then Liberia's most important industry, began to take second place in the national economy to the mining of iron ore. Iron ore was discovered only in the 1940s, in the mountainous area that forms the northern border with Guinea. Today iron ore mining is an important activity in four main areas—the most significant is around Mt. Nimba, and the other three are the Bomi Hills, the Mano Hills, and the Bong Range. The value of the iron ore exported from Liberia accounts for over half the country's total export earnings.

LIBERIANS

SINCE LIBERIA IS, in a sense, an artificially created country, the many ethnic groups that live within its borders are almost accidentally Liberian, and most of the tribal areas cross Liberian borders into other countries. Depending on what criteria one uses to define an ethnic group, there are between 16 and 28 ethnic groups in addition to the Americo-Liberians. Of these, just three—the Bassa, Dei, and Belle—are found only in Liberia. All the others exist in greater numbers in other countries.

Mainly because of this ethnic diversity, it is not easy to generalize about Liberians. A city dweller who lives in the capital and is aware of being a descendant of a 19th century family of freed slaves has a sense of identity that is quite different from that of, say, a Muslim rice farmer from the Kissi tribe in the interior of the country. What may be said of Liberians as a whole is that they are an open-hearted and warm people.

Typical Liberian teenagers, despite having grown up in a period of civil war with its widespread death and destruction, are far younger at heart than many of their contemporaries in North America or Western Europe. Adult Liberians retain a childlike sense of fun and enjoyment that many of their peers in other parts of the world have left behind in their rush to grow up. Even compared to people in other parts of Africa, Liberians are noted for their infectious enthusiasm for enjoyment.

About 42% of Liberia's population live in urban areas. The country is split quite clearly into two lifestyles—the traditional village life of the tribes and the urban Western-style market economy.

Above: **Liberians have a sense of fun and enjoyment despite the years of fighting that they have endured.**

Opposite: **A Belle girl with** *kaolin* **(white clay) decorations on her face and body.**

DEMOGRAPHICS

The population of Liberia, including refugees who have taken up residence in neighboring countries, is about 3 million, or about 49 persons per square mile. In 1991 at least half the population were refugees. The population is unevenly distributed, with most people living around Monrovia and in a stretch of land from Montserrado County to the Guinea border. The chief urban settlements are Monrovia, Buchanan, Edina, Greenville, Harper, Robertsport, and Marshall—all coastal towns. There are about 2,000 villages, mostly in central Liberia, the northwest, and close to Monrovia. In contrast, the southeastern forests are uninhabited. Putting aside population shifts caused by the war, the trend of movement is from rural areas to urban, especially to Monrovia. There are also population movements to the enclaves around rubber plantations and iron mines.

Monrovia's Carey Street. Liberia's population is concentrated in its cities.

The population of Liberia, which increased from about 758,000 in 1950 to 1.5 million in 1974, to the present 3 million, is one of the fastest growing in the world. One reason for this is the negligible emigration of Liberians. Other reasons for the increase are the high birthrate and decreased mortality rate as endemic diseases have been controlled in recent years. Even so, the infant mortality rate is high, at 153 per 1,000 live births, and the life expectancy is low—54 years for men and 56 years for women. This produces an unusual age distribution: over 43% of the population is under 15 years old and only 6% of the population is over 60. The average family size is five persons.

About 510,000 people are in the labor force; of these, 220,000 are part of the market economy and the rest work in the rural subsistence economy. Of the total population, 70.5% is engaged in agriculture, 10% in the service industry, and 4.5% in industry.

In 1990 non-Africans made up about 0.8% of the population.

Refugees fetch water from a well. The war has increased the number of refugees both in Liberia and in neighboring countries.

Bassa boys. The Bassa live along the coast and, like the Kru, make good sailors.

THE TRIBES

The government of Liberia recognizes 16 different tribes, although ethnolinguists put the number at around 28, based on language differences and cultural habits. The indigenous tribes can largely be divided into three ethnolinguistic groups, that is, groups of people who share a common language and customs.

THE KWA-SPEAKING PEOPLE The Kwa-speaking tribes include the Kru, Bassa, Dei, and Grebo. Their traditional homelands are the fertile plains extending along the coast from the Ivory Coast to Monrovia and beyond. The Kru (8% of the population) are well known as good seamen and traders. In the past they dealt in slaves and wore tattoos on their foreheads identifying themselves as Kru and warning people not to try to enslave them. The Bassa (16.3%) live in central Liberia. They live only in Liberia and, like the other members of this language group, have migrated in large numbers to the urban areas. The Dei (0.5%) are a small group. The Grebo (7.6%) occupy the extreme southeast of the country.

Two interior tribes—the Krahn (5.2%) and the Belle (0.5%)—also speak a language related to these groups, although they are traditionally agriculturists and hunter-gatherers rather than seafarers.

THE MANDE-SPEAKING PEOPLE The Mande speakers come from the north of the country and are indistinguishable from tribes of the same name in other West African countries such as Mali, Guinea, Sierra Leone, and the Ivory Coast. Eight tribes of this group live in Liberia—the

Mandingo, Vai, Gbandi, Kpelle, Loma, Mende, Gio, and Mano. Although they are grouped together due to the similarities in their language, they have very different cultures and traditions. The Mende (0.5%) have a strong tradition of masked devil dancing, while the Loma (5.3%) have historically been soldiers in the Frontier Force. The Mandingo (2.9%), most of whom are Muslim, are traders. The Kpelle (20.8%) are the most traditional of these tribes, having remained hunter-gatherers and farmers. The Vai (2.8%) are a coastal group with a literary tradition. They, too, are Muslim and most make their living through subsistence farming, fishing, and craftwork.

THE WEST ATLANTIC SPEAKERS The West Atlantic speakers are a small group of tribes composed of people from the interior who probably came to Liberia from the northwest. They make up about 8% of the population. They are mainly rice farmers, and many of them are Muslim.

The Gola and Kissi belong to this group. The Kissi inhabit a belt of hills at the point where Guinea, Liberia, and Sierra Leone meet. They cultivate rice in natural marshland and grow yams, sweet potatoes, and taro. They also grow and sell coffee and kola nuts. Their huts are round and built of clay, and villages are small with about 150 residents, all related. At the head of the village is the senior member of the family, who acts as the priest. The Kissi make stone statues of their ancestors. They are also famous for their currency, called "Kissi money"—small twisted iron bars, no longer in use.

A woman belonging to the Gola tribe, near Zorzor. The Gola are mainly rice farmers.

THE MAJOR TRIBAL GROUPS	
Bassa	16.3%
Belle	0.5%
Dei	0.5%
Gbandi	2.8%
Gola	4.7%
Grebo	7.6%
Kissi	3.4%
Kpelle	20.8%
Krahn	5.2%
Kru	8%
Loma	5.3%
Mandingo	2.9%
Mende	0.5%
Vai	2.8%
Other Liberian tribes	0.2%
Non-Liberian tribes	0.9%

THE AMERICO-LIBERIANS

Americo-Liberians are the descendants of the 12,000 people who founded Liberia, the freed slaves from the United States who settled there in the 19th century. Most of them migrated between 1820 and 1865. The term Americo-Liberian is avoided today, since it implies that this group is still a settler group and not really part of the country. Americo-Liberians make up about 1.5% of the population. They are chiefly urban and educated, with a distinct class system of a very wealthy elite who own estates or businesses, a middle class of clerical people, and a class of poor manual workers. The elite consist of about 1,500 people, 3.3% of the Americo-Liberian population.

The Americo-Liberian population has grown since the 19th century, either by natural growth or the integration of indigenous people into the group through marriage or adoption. Like their indigenous neighbors, Americo-Liberians followed the practice of taking in a local child as a servant, in exchange for support or cash for the parents. Such children were often adopted by the family and absorbed into its culture. Also, in the past many Americo-Liberian men followed the local custom of taking second wives. Children by those marriages were legally adopted.

The group also includes about 4,000 people called Congoes ("KON-gohs"), who are barely distinguishable from Americo-Liberians. These are the descendants of freed slaves taken from slaving ships captured by the US Navy when sailing from Africa to the Caribbean. "Congo" has become a pejorative term for all Americo-Liberians.

While most Americo-Liberians live in the major towns in the coastal plain, many of them have country houses well away from the cities. Before the 1990 coup the Americo-Liberians made up the bulk of the ruling elite in Liberia. They are largely Christian.

OTHERS

In addition to the Americo-Liberians and the various tribal groups that have always lived in Liberia, there are relatively newer and more temporary settlers who found Liberia's peace and stability an inducement to settle and trade. Liberia's constitution does not allow for non-blacks to become citizens, but people from many countries have become part of the social and cultural life of the country.

Many Ghanaians have settled in Liberia as semipermanent residents. They are chiefly people from the Fanti tribe and are traditionally fishermen who work the coastal shores. Many of the Fanti have settled in the towns, received an education, and become office workers, adopting the city lifestyle. The Fanti in Liberia are largely literate and make up about 0.5% of the population, making their ethnic group as large as some of the smaller indigenous tribes.

Another distinctive group is the Lebanese. Arab traders settled extensively throughout West Africa, and Liberia was no exception. Even in small towns in Liberia, there are stores and restaurants run by Lebanese. Although they are not allowed to become citizens, they have contributed much to the economy of the country.

Although people from many countries have settled in Liberia, the constitution allows only blacks to become citizens.

When the economy was flourishing, foreign companies were encouraged to invest in Liberian industry, and Americans, Spanish, Dutch, British, Germans, and Swedes worked in Liberia, particularly in Monrovia. They worked as professional advisors, technical experts, teachers, or missionaries. They were evacuated at the beginning of the civil war.

NATIONAL DRESS

When the early settlers came from the United States they emulated the dress of the wealthy plantation owners of the South, including frock coats, top hats, and cravats. These days most Liberians wear Western-style dress adapted for the humidity and heat.

Traditional dress for women is a wide-necked blouse called a *bubba*, often in colorful designs such as tie-dye, and a full-length sarong, called a *lappas*, in equally vivid colors. At one time, portraits of famous African leaders were popular on clothes. Most women wear a headdress made of a scarf tied in elaborate ways. Men wear loose, brightly colored shirts over Western-style cotton trousers.

When they take part in dance festivals, Liberians often cover themselves in white clay and wear long skirts made from grass, dyed and woven tunics, beads, and colorful headdresses.

Western-style clothes adapted for the heat and humidity are popular in Liberia, especially in the cities.

SOME FAMOUS LIBERIANS

William Tubman, born in 1895 in Harper, was of Americo-Liberian descent. In 1943 he became president, sponsored by the ruling True Whig Party. He was conscious of the divisions in his country, where a tiny elite controlled most of the wealth and power, and began unifying all tribal groups and encouraging tribal leaders to join the national government. He also carried out a policy of open door economics, encouraging foreign investment. He died in 1971.

Another famous Liberian is George Weah, who has played for the French football team Paris St. Germain and for AC Milan. In 1995 he was voted Europe's Best African Player by the French magazine *Onze Mondial*.

William Tubman is regarded as the founder of modern Liberia.

CHARLES TAYLOR

Charles Taylor was born in 1947 into a fairly prosperous family and was educated in the United States. Entering politics back in Liberia in 1980, he became an assistant minister in the People's Redemption Council, a position he held for three years. Political problems led him to flee the country, and he was held for extradition in the United States. In 1984 he escaped from jail in Massachusetts, and in 1985 he founded his own party (NPFL).

It was Taylor's army that precipitated the civil war when he took up arms against the government in 1989, and his party was one of the chief signatories at the peace accord in Nigeria in 1995. Taylor himself narrowly escaped an assassination attempt in 1996, which he blamed on a rival faction. In July 1997 Taylor was elected president of the country.

LIFESTYLE

FOR DECADES LIBERIA WAS the most stable and flourishing country in Africa. While coups and military governments seemed to be commonplace throughout the continent, Liberia prospered. When stability ended with Doe's coup in 1980, the causes could be seen in the basic social structure of the country. Liberia was, and still is, divided into two quite distinct ways of life—the tribal life of the villages and the Westernized urban life, which has a social hierarchy with a small elite of wealthy people at the top. A decade or so of war and coups has had little effect on that division. As the war recedes and stability begins to return to the towns, the refugees are returning to their homes, many of which have been devastated. But the inequalities that brought about 15 years or so of problems and intertribal warfare still exist. All the factions that have fought over Monrovia have fought for their group to have the biggest share of the profits, not to bring about a fairer system.

Opposite: **Villagers make string and raffia out of coconut palm leaves, which they weave into baskets.**

Left: **Liberians who fled their homeland during the civil strife are beginning to return.**

57

CITY LIFE

Visitors to Monrovia in 1980 might have been forgiven for believing themselves to be in a new state of the United States. The currency was the US dollar, the policemen wore secondhand New York Police Department summer uniforms, and signs outside the larger towns announced their names as New Georgia, Maryland, and Louisiana. On Saturday nights the night clubs and bars were lit up, while on Sundays Baptist choirs could be heard. Anyone turning on the radio would hear Voice of America.

Now things are different, largely due to the impact of the war and the changes brought about by indigenous African governments. The Liberian dollar has replaced the US dollar, and the night life is quieter.

Monrovia is a small capital by Western standards, with an area of about five square miles. It has an interesting mix of architecture, with old

The capital has sprawling shantytowns filled with homes made out of cardboard and corrugated iron.

Southern US-style mansions and bungalows, now dilapidated, alongside more modern high-rise buildings. Besides these are traditional African huts as well as shantytowns. The population is made up of tribal groups living in small communities. Each ethnic group has developed its own churches and social structures.

Members of the same ethnic group often share the same type of work. The Kru, for example, who live in the coastal towns, work mainly as sailors or as stevedores on the docks, although some have joined the teaching and medical professions, the civil service, and politics. They are organized into clanlike groups, and an organization called the Kru Corporation, founded in 1916, handles disputes between tribespeople and their employers.

The towns have people living in extreme poverty close to others who are very wealthy. The population of the towns is young and there is a high proportion of males to females, as young men migrate from rural areas to the cities in search of work.

Towns have developed along major roads to the big mining and farming estates. Zorzor, for example, is on the main road to Sierra Leone. Kpelle and Loma take their farm produce there. It has a hospital funded and supported by the Lutheran Church of America, a teacher-training college, and some small industries. It is a quiet town, depending on trade and foreign-funded projects, such as the hospital and a leper colony. The church is the center of social events. Two-story concrete housing blocks predominate in the modern parts of the town, while typical older homes are rectangular and one-story, their walls made of plaited mats or mud and wattle, with tin roofs.

Pedestrians and vehicles jostle for space on Monrovia's Randall Street.

Students at a school in Lofa County. Educational standards in Liberia are high by African standards, thanks largely to a well-developed system of schools and the efforts of US Peace Corps volunteers who teach in many areas.

EDUCATION

In the early years of settlement by Americo-Liberians, education for the settlers' children was considered of paramount importance. Americo-Liberian children were educated in locally established schools for entrance to professions such as law, theology, and medicine. After elementary school they went to the United States, Europe, or neighboring African countries to complete their education.

There was no provision for indigenous children to go to school, even those living close to the settlements. As time passed, schools were set up by various missionary groups. These provided the only education available to indigenous children. By 1939, private or mission schools provided three-quarters of Liberia's elementary education.

Little changed until after World War II, when the government became aware of the need to educate the indigenous children. In 1961 a system was set up that lasted until the civil war began. Nursery school was followed by six years of elementary school, three years of junior high school, and high school. By the late 1960s, 50% of schools were government financed and run; the rest were privately run facilities and mission schools, in equal numbers. Today slightly less than 50% of schools are financed by missionary societies or by the big mining companies for their workers' children. Instruction covers literacy, mathematics, science, and work-oriented programs such as cooking, agriculture, and manual skills.

Today, education is compulsory for children 6 to 16 years old. Elementary and secondary education is free. In practice, though, only about half the school-age children attend elementary school and about 20% attend secondary school, although the secondary school population has increased eightfold since the 1960s. Rural children have a poor attendance record, since schools in rural areas are widely scattered and there is no reliable daily transportation; nor do the schools have dormitory facilities. In addition, the use of English for instruction has made education difficult for rural children. In both rural and city schools the dropout rate is very high: only one-quarter of children who start first grade finish sixth grade. Textbooks are expensive, and it is difficult to get good teachers with the country torn apart by war. Fewer girls attend school than boys, and they often start at a much later age so that by fourth grade they leave to get married. About 25% of young people are literate. These figures were much lower during the height of the war.

Further education is largely provided by the University of Liberia in Monrovia, Cuttington University College in Suakoko, and a college of science and technology in Harper. There are several teacher-training colleges and a school for paramedics in Monrovia.

Students at a Catholic school in Gardnersville, a suburb of Monrovia.

Handicraft on sale at the leprosy center in Ghunta. Leper colonies are often self-financing, having craft centers where the inmates make and sell objects such as baskets and wood carvings.

WELFARE

The welfare system, already overburdened and underfunded, was seriously shaken by the effects of war. Before the war there were 89 doctors, 908 nurses, and 5 dentists in Liberia. The country currently has 85 hospitals, with 15 beds for every 10,000 persons.

Many diseases that are fairly easy to eradicate elsewhere are endemic in Liberia, due to the disruptions caused by the war and other factors. Malaria is a serious problem. The disease is spread by mosquitoes, which breed in stagnant water. It can be tackled by treating mosquito breeding grounds and by taking medication once the disease is contracted. Both these tasks are difficult to undertake in a rainy country such as Liberia, which has minimal infrastructure even in peacetime. Leprosy is an easily spread bacterial infection, but it is possible to make leprosy patients noninfectious with continuous medication. Liberia has leprosy centers where infected people can live and earn a living.

Smallpox and yellow fever are viral diseases that can be prevented by immunization. They are less threatening in Liberia than they once were, but once again the disruption caused by the civil war has increased their incidence. Tuberculosis is another bacterial infection that has not been eradicated. Yaws, a skin infection, has been brought largely under control by a program conducted by the World Health Organization.

Poor-quality drinking water is a major problem in Liberia. Less than 40% of the population has access to safe drinking water, and with the war this figure has worsened. Unsafe drinking water can cause many diseases, the major killer being dysentery, caused by bacteria or parasites spread through contaminated food or water. Schistosomiasis is also caused by a parasite spread through unclean drinking water, particularly river water. It kills slowly, destroying the internal organs, where the eggs of the parasite build up. Other major diseases in Liberia are trypanosomiasis, or sleeping sickness, intestinal worms, and elephantiasis.

Poor diet is an important factor in susceptibility to disease and, therefore, the high infant mortality rate. Measles, easily cured in developed countries, is another major contributor to infant mortality.

Government expenditure on health care is 5% of the national budget, that is, US$7 per head per annum. Although this figure is relatively high by African standards, the expenditure is concentrated on the urban areas. The most extensive health care facilities are found in the Monrovia region and the industrial areas.

In the village of Gahtar, antimalarial tablets are distributed. Children and adults swallow them with enthusiasm.

Every village has a pa-laver hut, where disputes are settled.

TRIBAL AND VILLAGE LIFE

Given Liberia's several ethnic groups and ways of life, it is difficult to get an accurate picture of the typical village or community. Usually the villages are small. Often, but not always, they are ethnically homogeneous, and the villagers' lifestyles are usually based on farming and hunting.

In the past Liberia was largely covered with dense forest, and people lived in small family units of a few huts in a clearing that they had hacked out for themselves. They grew a few crops and hunted and gathered the fruits of the forest. New areas of forest had to be constantly cleared, as the soil was not very fertile, and abandoned patches quickly returned to dense scrubland. Footpaths linked each family's clearing with those of their near relatives. Long journeys were hazardous and not entered into lightly.

Modern villages are larger but are still made up of distantly related families. The village site is chosen for its good drainage, perhaps on high ground that can be defended easily, and near a stream for water—but not too close, since the spirits of the dead are thought to live in streams. Houses are circular huts built on a frame of poles. Through the poles are woven flexible branches, and plastered onto the branches is a fine mud collected from deserted termite nests. A conical roof extends over the house walls, forming a verandah. The roof tiles are split oil palm leaves.

Within each village is an open space for meetings and festivals, and a palaver ("puh-LAV-er") hut where disputes are discussed and the village elders meet. It has a raised floor and palm-thatched roof but no walls, so that open meetings can be held there.

Larger villages, perhaps evolving along the roads built by foreign companies or along the old trading routes, are more sophisticated. They have rectangular huts with corrugated iron roofs, and a grand market day when people from the smaller villages congregate and the whole day is spent trading. Mandingo traders travel around the various village markets, which are intentionally held on different days.

Villages along the coast have a greater Western influence. The religions there are Christianity, Islam, and native religions. Fishing is an important part of their economy. The Kru who live there build boats and catch fish to eat or sell. The women grow cassava, peanuts, and vegetables. Coastal people rely more on trade than do villagers in the interior.

People from the smaller villages go to the larger ones on market day— to sell or to shop.

THE FAMILY AND MARRIAGE

City dwellers in Liberia have Westernized attitudes toward marriage and the family. They believe in monogamous marriages, and weddings sometimes include church services. The couple often meet at church or at a dance, and once the decision to marry has been made, they save for their new home.

Customs in the rural areas are quite different, as there are several forms of relationships between men and women, some of an informal nature and others involving serious bargaining between the two families and cash exchanges.

In traditional African society both children and wives are considered assets—women can cook, work in the fields, look after children, and sell produce in the markets. Children, too, increase a man's wealth by the future advantages they will give him—daughters can be sold for a bride price and sons help to protect the group and can work in the fields. The children owe a debt to their parents that the latter can call on in their old age.

Most men have at least two wives, each with her own hut, belongings, and children. In traditional Kpelle society it is the first wife who chooses the next one, often a friend or sister, perhaps one who is widowed. The first wife usually welcomes the help and company of another wife. There is no shame in being the second or third wife, and there is no legal distinction among the children of different wives. Very rich men have several wives and children and sometimes lend their wives to poorer men in exchange for their political support, manual labor, or some other favor.

Divorce is simple—a matter of arguing in front of the village elders over who gets what. Divorce is not a shameful affair. A man or woman who finds out that his or her partner is carrying on a secret affair can get compensation for the loss of work or possessions that this represents. The extramarital relationship is not considered an immoral act, as it might be in Western society, but a threat to the economic structure of the family.

Opposite: **An urban bride arrives at the gate of her church.**

BRIDE PRICE

In some tribal groups children are betrothed at a very young age in a contract arranged by both sets of parents. This usually involves the payment of bride price or "brideservice," that is, work promised in lieu of payment. Very powerful men can offer political patronage as their bride price. Older men can afford to pay a bride price for their wife because they have savings or have built up wealth. This might be cash or livestock or even cloth, palm wine, nuts, or some other valuable object. Young men must offer some service to their future in-laws, such as work in their fields. Unless he is wealthy, at his marriage a man puts himself in debt to his in-laws for an indefinite period. If a man is very rich and powerful, people will be glad to give their daughters to him in return for his favors. Among the Kpelle, men like this are called *to nuu* ("toh NEW"), which the Kpelle translate as "big shot." Parents do not easily give up their daughters, since they represent potential wealth, and so there are many stories warning young girls about choosing the wrong husband.

Bassa girls in a Sande bush school. Modern Sande schools teach girls practical skills and not witchcraft and the use of herbs, as the earlier ones did.

SECRET SOCIETIES

Most tribal people in Liberia take part in some kind of secret society. The two major ones are the Sande and Poro secret societies for women and men respectively. As people pass through the various stages in the society they learn new rituals and lore that are a mystery to the uninitiated. Bush schools are held every year to induct young people. The Poro schools teach boys practical skills such as building liana bridges, handling wives, and building houses, but they also teach tribal law, correct behavior to elders, and secrets of the religion. At one time, endurance tests such as scarring were part of the course, and elaborate festivals marked the start and end of the school.

The Sande schools used to teach girls cooking, the mysteries of marriage, childbirth, witchcraft, and the use of herbs, but now they are less magic-oriented and ritualistic and more cultural and practical.

There are some secret societies that are exclusive and, unlike the others, have a strong affiliation with the darker aspects of magic. The Leopard

Society is one such group, now outlawed, whose members were said to have power over life and death. Another group is the Snake Society, whose rituals involve the handling of poisonous snakes.

The old, elite families had a powerful males-only semisecret society—the Ancient, Free and Accepted Masonic Lodge of Liberia. It was founded in 1867, and by 1980 when it was decimated in the coup, it had about 17 branches in Liberia. Virtually all the social and political leaders were members, and the Lodge had a powerful influence on government decisions. The Masons were bitterly resented by the newly emerging young professionals of tribal origin in the 1970s and 1980s. There was a women's version of the Lodge—the Order of the Eastern Star of Africa.

The Masonic Temple, one of Monrovia's landmark buildings, was looted and burned in the 1980 coup.

RELIGION

SOME STATISTICS PUT Christianity as the most popular religion in Liberia, while others maintain it is the least popular. What is definite is that there are three main faiths: Christianity, Islam, and traditional African religions. Christianity, the most recent introduction, was brought to Liberia by the early Americo-Liberian settlers and encouraged by missionary groups. Islam, both Sunni and Shi'a, was introduced in West Africa by caravan merchants crossing the Sahara from about the 11th century. Later, it was spread by such groups as the Mandingo.

The oldest forms of religious belief in Liberia are the indigenous religions, of which animism is a common aspect. They possess belief in a supreme god, but spiritual power is usually experienced through everyday things or beings that are seen to be endowed with a supernatural element. Witchcraft is accepted by most people and practiced regardless of religious conviction.

Opposite: **A Bassa girl with her brother. Many of the Bassa are Christian.**

Left: **A church in Harper. There are no reliable estimates for the religious affiliations in Liberia, but Christianity is one of the three main religions.**

A Gio *zoe* scatters rice in an animist ritual.

TRIBAL RELIGIONS

Some official figures put animism as the religion of 90% of Liberia's population. Although the different groups' religious beliefs vary, the animistic religions of Liberia do have some features in common. Animists believe in a spiritual world where things around them—trees, rocks, streams, virtually anything—are imbued with life and the power to cause harm or good. All objects encountered must therefore be treated with reverence. Objects can also be called on to help the individual, usually through the aid of someone called a *zoe* ("ZOH"), the animist equivalent of a priest, doctor, and medium.

Animists believe in three gods—the creator, the ancestor, and the nature spirit. Of immediate importance to them are the latter two, which include different aspects of the spirit world.

Animists rely on the spirits of their ancestors to affect their own lives. The most recently deceased make the most powerful spirits. After death, very important people are worshiped not only by their relatives but also by members of their village. As the generations pass, the older spirits fade away into a group that is recognized in worship but not considered harmful.

A nature spirit is the spirit of a particular rock, tree, or river, which animists believe has the power to affect the lives of the people living near it. Animists give the object a name and try to appease it with sacrifices. A spirit may make an appearance in its true form, in which case viewers can be harmed or benefited, depending on how they treat it.

TOTEMISM

One aspect of the animistic religion can be seen in the Kpelle tribe. They practice a custom called totemism, where an individual has a special relationship with a particular object. It represents a magical force that stands behind the individual (or in some cases the tribe) and guides and protects them. A totem might be a particular species of animal or plant, or even a rock. To the Kpelle, each tribe's totem is the place where the ancestors reside. In the case of an individual, his or her totem might be a wild cat, a boar, or some other animal. Appearances of that animal can be taken as an omen. A father can pass his totem on to his son or a mother to her daughter. Most children are given a plant totem at birth. People with the same totem consider themselves to be kin, so a boy from one tribe whose totem is the leopard would feel kinship with another boy from a different tribe or village with the same totem.

One possible reason why different figures are given for the various religious affiliations is that many tribal people hold two faiths: that of their tribal traditions and a new religion—Christianity or Islam.

The villagers' totems are kept in a totem hut.

73

MAGIC

Animists believe that ancestral spirits and spirits that reside in objects of nature can be used to bring about change. They appease these spirits through rituals and the offering of gifts. The practice is called magic or witchcraft, and the people who practice it are called magicians or medicine men.

These specialists, or *zoe,* are believed to be able to create medicine from herbs or animal tissue, which can be eaten, carried about as amulets, or hidden near people to affect them in a positive or negative way. Some of these are genuine herbal remedies, while others call on the belief of the people taking part in the magic to make it work. Sometimes the medicine calls for human flesh or organs.

Most urbanized tribespeople claim they no longer believe in magic, but there have been cases in recent history of powerful political figures using it. For instance, when President Samuel Doe was assassinated, he was left to die with his arms tied because of the belief of those who were around him that if he were freed his spirit would be released to gain power over another body.

CHRISTIANITY

The first Christians to arrive in Liberia were the American settlers. Their denominations were the United Methodists and the Liberian Baptist Convention. The first director of the colony at Cape Mesurado, later renamed Monrovia, was Jehudi Ashmun, a Methodist minister. Methodism derives from the teachings of John Wesley, an 18th century British Christian. Several separate black Methodist churches were formed, most of which disapproved of the attempt to resettle former slaves in Africa.

Baptists belong to a Christian church originating in England in the 17th century. Baptist churches are founded on the belief that the church is only for true believers, who must be baptized when they accept the belief and who must give testimony of their faith. There is no church hierarchy. A Baptist church is simple, as is its service. Baptists believe in the separation of church and state. Having said that, the ruling classes of Liberia were for many years dominated by Baptists and Methodists. In the early days typical services in both churches were evangelical revival meetings, with singing and the giving of testimony. As time passed, the services grew more subdued and formal.

The Catholic Church, the Lutheran Church, and the Episcopal Church arrived later. The last became a prestigious organization, adopted by many of the educated elite as well as educated Vai and tribal students at Cuttington University College. The Roman Catholic Church set up missions among the Kru, Grebo, and Krahn and made many converts among those tribes. Lutherans have converted many of the Kpelle and Loma.

Above: **Sunday service in St. Peter's Lutheran Church in a suburb of Monrovia. Soldiers of Samuel Doe's government massacred more than 600 civilians in this church in July 1990.**

Opposite: **A medicine man displays his tools.**

INDIGENOUS AFRICAN CHRISTIANITY

Over the years, the mainstream churches with American origins have become less active and other Christian churches have emerged. Congregations of the newer churches tend to be ethnically homogeneous, that is, made up of only one tribe. The Liberian Assemblies of God, for example, has missions among the city Kru. An indigenous African church, the Church of the Lord (Aladura) ("AL-ad-ER-ah") has faith healing, African music, and a lively atmosphere.

Members of the indigenous churches tend to be manual workers with little formal education, whereas members of mainstream churches are wealthy, literate, and often from politically powerful families.

THE CHURCH OF THE LORD (ALADURA)

The Church of the Lord (Aladura) originated among the Yoruba people of Nigeria in the early 20th century. The name Aladura means "Owners of Prayer." The church rejected both Western medicine and African traditional charms as agents of healing, and concentrated on the "laying on of hands" and prayer.

The Aladura church began with a small group of Anglicans during an influenza epidemic in 1918, when many people were dying. It was inspired by American churches such as the Philadelphia Faith Tabernacle Church, which practiced faith healing. By the 1920s, when the Aladura was forced to leave the Anglican Church, it had become very popular.

By the 1960s the church had spread to Ghana, Togo, Liberia, Sierra Leone, and Benin. In Liberia it is a church of the urban areas and is favored by city Kpelle, Bassa, and Kru. Today there are several Aladura congregations in New York and London.

ISLAM

Indigenous people have converted to Islam and Christianity in more or less equal numbers. Islam came to Liberia through the early caravan traders and was spread by the Mandingo, of whom around 90% profess Islam. The Vai have also converted to Islam in large numbers, as have other tribes such as the Gola, Mende, Kissi, and Gbandi in the northwest.

The form of Islam practiced in Liberia is largely Sunni, or orthodox Islam. The Sunnis acknowledge the first four caliphs as the rightful successors of Prophet Mohammed. The Shi'a sect is represented by the Lebanese, who work in Liberia as traders. Shi'as believe Mohammed was succeeded by his son-in-law, Ali, and that Ali will one day return. A small number of Liberian Muslims profess Ahmadiya Islam, a heretical form not considered to be the true faith by other sects.

Islam originated in Arabia in the seventh century following the teachings of the Prophet Mohammed. Muslims believe in one God, in angels who bring His word to the people, and in the 28 prophets who received God's message. One of those prophets, they believe, was Jesus Christ, an ordinary man. Others are Abraham, David, Moses, and writers of the New Testament, all figures known in Christianity. Muslims also believe in a final day of judgement, when they will hear the sound of Angel Asrafil blowing a trumpet. There are five pillars of Islam, or things a Muslim must do: declaration of the one true God with Mohammed as his prophet, prayer, fasting, pilgrimage to Mecca, and giving alms to the poor.

The Mandingo mosque in Gbarnga. Islam was spread throughout Liberia by the Mandingo, who are traditionally traveling traders.

77

LANGUAGE

LIBERIA HAS AN EXTREMELY complex system of languages. Its indigenous languages can be divided into three main groups, all belonging to the Niger-Congo group of languages: the West Atlantic or Mel, Kwa, and Mande, the last of which is the most popular, spoken by over a million people. The Niger-Congo languages account for 1,000 languages in sub-Saharan Africa. In addition, there is the official language, which is English, and various versions or pidgins of English that are spoken around the country.

The three main language groups consist of more than 30 subgroups and dialects. Some groups, such as the Vai, have also adopted Arabic. This makes communication quite a problem. Intertribal communication is often made through a common root language or in pidgin English. It is common for Liberians to be multilingual.

It is thought that the Kru, considered to be good sailors, have given their name to the English word for men who work on a ship—crew.

Opposite: **There are over 30 languages and dialects in Liberia, but English is the main language of communication in the towns.**

Left: **A village school in Upper Lofa. In rural areas of Liberia few children encounter any English.**

ENGLISH

English is the official government language and the language of education. It is the mother tongue of about 2.5% of the population, but it is spoken in one form or another as a second language by around 1.5 million people. It differs sharply from the other forms of African English in that it uses American word choices. For example, the terms used in reference to the secondary school system are high school, junior high school, grades, vacation, graduation—rather than the British English terms used in other African countries. In Nigeria you buy "biscuits" in a "shop," whereas in Liberia you buy "cookies" in a "store." Indigenous African names are becoming more common, but European first and last names have long been accepted as normal. This tradition goes back to the freed slaves who brought with them non-African names. Indeed, every one of Liberia's presidents had or has a European last name.

Right: **English is widely spoken and understood in Liberia, particularly in the urban areas.**

Opposite: **In addition to standard American English, many pidgin forms exist in Liberia.**

In addition to the standard American English of broadcasting, government, the courts, and international business, there are many pidgin forms. The English language came to Liberia with the Americo-Liberians, many of whom spoke an African-American Creole form of English when they arrived. This evolved into an amalgamation much closer to the indigenous languages than, say, the Krio pidgin language of neighboring Sierra Leone, which had only one wave of pidginization. In Monrovia there are many pidgins, each one influenced by the mother tongue of the tribe. In some cases, for example the Monrovian pidgin called Kepama, the pidgin has become the mother tongue and is spoken more easily than the original language.

BIG SHOTS

The various tribes of Liberia had a social structure that respected a certain number of wealthy men who grew very powerful within tribal groups, had many wives, and could call on several men for assistance during conflicts with other groups. When people with these customs came in contact with English-speaking people, the nearest translation for such a person was "big shot." In English it is almost a term of abuse to describe someone who shows off wealth, but it does not have that connotation in Liberian English.

The Americo-Liberians fitted the indigenous people's ideas of what a big shot was and so were given the kind of respect reserved for tribal leaders. Big shots were expected to show off their wealth and use it for political purposes. After the 1980 coup, many big shots fell foul of the new regime and were killed, and it became less socially acceptable, if not positively dangerous, to be a big shot, because it represented a challenge to the government of the day— Samuel Doe.

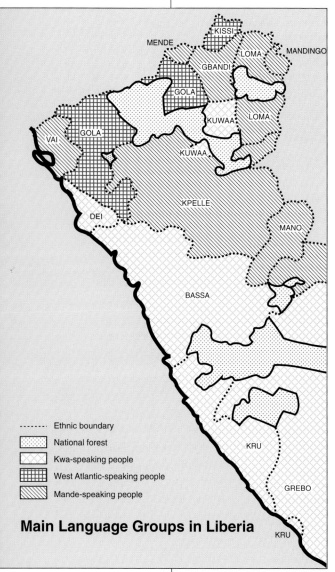

Ethnic boundary
National forest
Kwa-speaking people
West Atlantic-speaking people
Mande-speaking people

Main Language Groups in Liberia

REGIONAL LANGUAGES

The Mande languages are not restricted to Liberia but extend into Mali, Guinea, the Ivory Coast, and Sierra Leone. In Liberia they are spoken by the Vai, Mandingo, Gbandi, Kpelle, Loma, Mende, Gio, and Mano. Most Mande speakers live in the north and east, with only the Vai living on the coast. Not all Mande speakers can understand one another.

The Kwa languages number around 73, most of them not spoken in Liberia. They are spoken by the Bassa (the largest ethnic group in Monrovia), Kru, Dei, Belle, Krahn, Kuwaa, and Grebo. Kwa speakers inhabit the coastline and the south of the country. Typical of the Kwa languages is the use of tones to give context to a word. The closeness of Kwa languages can be seen in the word for water, which is *ni* ("NEE") in Bassa, Kru, and Kuwaa. Similarly, the word for tree is *chu* ("CHU") in all three languages.

The West Atlantic speakers are the Gola and Kissi of Liberia and Sierra Leone. These tribes, the oldest inhabitants of Liberia, live in the north. Their languages form part of a group of 23 spoken around West Africa, the most important of which is Fulani. Like Chinese, these languages use tones to indicate meaning.

LINGUA FRANCAS

The main intertribal language is pidgin English, but there are also several tribal languages at a local level. For example, in northern and western Liberia all three of the main language groups exist in close proximity. Most people speak their own language and at least one of the other two language families, so that as long as three people are speaking they can be mutually understood.

In regions like this, in particular the area northwest of Monrovia, some indigenous languages are disappearing as the people adopt not English, but one of the other native languages. The Dei, for example, have taken up the Vai language at home as well as in business. Malinke ("mah-LINK-ee"), the language spoken by the Mandingo, has become a lingua franca because of the Mandingos' traditional role as traveling traders.

In some unusual cases the speakers of one language can understand another language but cannot be understood by speakers of the latter. For example, the Gbee speakers of Nimba County can understand the language of the Bassa but cannot be understood by them.

In many villages, people speaking different languages live happily side by side.

ACCENTS AND DIFFERENT MEANINGS

While it is acknowledged that Liberians speak a form of American English, American *kwi* ("KWEE," pidgin for foreigner) in Monrovia would have a hard time understanding what the person on the street was saying, although the former would be clearly understood. Many final sounds of words are not sounded, and a great many others are slurred. There are also some differences in usage that might be confusing. For example, many words have the suffix "o," so cheap becomes "cheap-o." Buses, cars, motorbikes, in fact any wheeled vehicle, is a "car." The word "palaver" is commonly used to mean a discussion, while in English it means a lot of fuss about nothing. And if you want to congratulate someone, you must say "thank you!"

Above: **Schoolchildren in the towns receive instruction in English.**

Below: **Vai script. The Vai were the first people in Liberia to invent a usable written language.**

WRITTEN LANGUAGES

In many cases the first written form of any African language came about through the efforts of missionaries, particularly Lutherans, who created a written form so that they could bring the word of the Bible to the tribes. In Liberia this was not the case. The vast number of subdialects made the work of the missionaries very difficult, since what might be intelligible to one group would make no sense to a neighboring village.

A script was developed for the Kpelle and alphabets for some other languages, but the first usable written language was invented by the Vai for their language. In the early 19th century a Vai named Dualu Bukele created a script for their language. It came into common use and was the basis for written versions of other languages. The script is not an alphabet but rather a syllabary. It has about 240 characters, each standing for a different vowel/consonant combination. Originally used to keep records of births, deaths, and marriages, and never used by women, the script is now used only by elderly men and is passed on to interested scholars. It was never taught in schools. Before the advent of English, the Vai script was used by the Loma, Kpelle, and Mende in their record keeping. During World War II, German intelligence officers used the Vai script to pass coded messages.

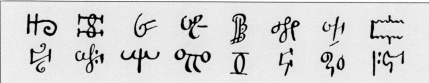

OTHER INFLUENCES

Early explorers of the region included the Portuguese, who gave names to some of Liberia's geographic features. The Mesurado River, for example, was named by the Portuguese and means "measured" or "quiet," probably because the mouth of the river is calm. The Gallinas River also has a Portuguese name meaning "hens."

The names of the St. John and St. Paul rivers have been anglicized, but they were originally Portuguese names. But Cess River comes from the Portuguese word *cestor,* meaning basket (probably after the basket-wielding fisherwomen the explorers saw there), the Sanguin River runs red during a flood (*sanguin* is Portuguese for red), and the Cavalla River has plenty of mackerel (mackerel is *caballa* in Portuguese). The name for the region of Liberia bordering on the Gulf of Guinea—the Grain Coast—also comes from the Portuguese, who named it for the grains of melegueta pepper they found growing there.

Liberian proverbs teach truths by relating it to their daily lives: *"He who steps in first shows the depth of the current"* means it is wise to stay back and watch others before acting, since what happens to them can teach one what to do. *"One does not throw a stick after the snake has gone"* is advice to seize opportunity when it occurs.

TALKING DRUMS

Common throughout West Africa, the talking drums were an early form of communication in Liberia. They are shaped like an hourglass, with skins covering both ends. The skins are connected by tightly stretched rawhide cords. The expert drum player can alter the sound of the drum by stretching or releasing these cords, thus creating a series of tones similar to the tonal languages of Liberia.

The drummers learned set series of beats and tones, which became a kind of Morse code but corresponded to the pattern of the actual words in a way that Morse code does not. A talking-drum player made it his life's work. The sound of the drums carried over long distances, and messages could be relayed over hundreds of miles in a very short time.

ARTS

IN TRADITIONAL LIBERIAN CULTURE the arts, leisure, religion, and festivals coincide in the colorful pageants and festivals of village life. In modern Liberian society the arts include literature and music with tribal and Western influences.

LITERATURE

Traditional literature arrived in Liberia with the ancestors of the Kpelle and Kru as they migrated across Africa from Sudan. They brought with them stories, parables, and proverbs, as well as legends of their ancestors' lives. The oral tradition was passed down by the fireside, in the bush schools, and in the meeting place of the village, where festivals celebrating the ancient stories were held. Although most tribes had no form of written language, the stories survived, but each time they were told they were altered a little, or some new ideas were added, so the stories grew in the telling.

One example of an ancient story is the Woi epic (refer to page 108), which is told by a professional storyteller. Every storyteller has his or her own way of telling it, but the basic events are the same. If everyone is having a good time, the Woi epic storytelling session may extend beyond just one evening. Many of the events in the tale are comic, and current events are often drafted into the story to give it a topical element.

In modern times anthropologists have recorded many of the oral stories, but as tribal living gradually gives way to an urban lifestyle the stories will fade away and lose their usefulness.

Above: **Folktales are handed down at informal gatherings, such as this one of Gio villagers.**

Opposite: **The *saa saa*, made out of a hollowed out and dried gourd, is an important part of the Vai musical ensemble.**

At the conclusion
of the novel Uncle
Tom's Cabin by
Harriet Beecher
Stowe, one of the
main characters
leaves the United
States for the
freedom of Liberia.

AMERICO-LIBERIAN LITERATURE

When the freed slaves sailed to Africa and settled in Liberia, they brought with them a complex cultural system. When their ancestors were taken to the United States or the Caribbean they were separated from others who spoke their language and knew their stories. The chances of their being with others from their own tribe were low. So they learned a common language, and the stories they brought with them from America became amalgamated into a new culture, intermingled with the adopted culture of their new home in Liberia. The people who settled in Liberia in the early 19th century had a culture that included 200 years of remembered African culture and was largely Christian, democratic, and literate.

The new settlers could read and write, and they had as their literary background the hymns and religious texts of Christianity. Their early literary efforts were a reaction to their pioneering status. Their lives were hard: they were trying to make a new and better life for themselves, but they discovered a country where African people traded slaves, there was constant intertribal warfare, and survival demanded a fight against the elements. The literary products of this were religious poetry and collected pulpit narrations, all with the common theme of their need to rely on God to see them through the difficult times.

As the two cultures—Americo-Liberian and African—have gradually assimilated ideas from each other, a new Liberian literature has emerged, which parallels the emergence of black literature in English across Africa. A journal called *Kaafa* ("KAH-feh") publishes short stories by Liberian writers, while for a time a Liberian publisher called Liberian Literary and Educational Publications was active in Monrovia. Some successful writers of the last few decades are Robert Brown, a lecturer at the University of Liberia who has written novels and short stories; Elizabeth Mitchel, a writer of essays and short stories as well as a short novel; R. Sylvanus Corker, who writes short stories and worked in the Liberian embassy in Washington; and Wilton G.S. Sankawulo, a novelist and short story writer who was briefly chair of the Council of State.

The first Liberian novel was called Love in Ebony *and was written by Charles Cooper in the late 19th century.*

AN 1836 POEM

Here is part of a poem by Americo-Liberian Hilary Teague, written in 1836:

> We sing the wondrous deeds of Him
> Who rides upon the sky;
> His name is God, the glorious theme
> Is sung by saints on high.

After a few stanzas praising God, she gets down to the story she has to tell:

> We were by those beset around,
> Who craved to drink our blood,
> Whose malice, hatred knew no bound,
> Whose hearts of love were void.

> The savage yell, the dreadful cry,
> Fell on our frightened ear,
> The gleaming spear, the clam'ring throng,
> With terror did appear.

The poem carries on in a similar vein and style, with God eventually calming the savages. It is written in the language of 19th century hymns, for example, "We were by those beset around." The poem gives some idea of the reaction of the settlers to what must have been a frightening savagery around them.

FOLKTALES

Common throughout Africa are the spider stories, and Liberia has its own versions of these. Ananse ("ah-NAN-say") the spider is a clever trickster, but his cleverness often brings about the wrong result and he usually gets caught in the end. The spider stories found their way into American culture by way of the slaves brought from Africa.

Another set of stories kept alive in the oral tradition are legends about ancestors. These stories probably began at the funeral of some great leader, where those at the celebration would improvise and probably exaggerate the stories of battles fought or animals killed. If the stories were good, bits would be remembered and repeated at the next celebration, and so on. Proverbs were another part of the oral tradition and were used to pass on the culture and values of the tribe.

THE GREEDY SPIDER

This story of Ananse the spider is told to Liberian children to warn them about the dangers of greed:

Ananse was invited to two village feasts, but he feared that if he went to one he would miss the other. So he tied two pieces of rope around his body and told each village chief to pull on the rope when his feast was ready. That way he could be there for both feasts. But it so happened that they both began at the same time. Each village elder pulled the rope from his village to call Ananse. Ananse, who had been sleeping under a tree between the two villages, could not move. One rope pulled him one way, and the other rope pulled him the other. When he did not arrive at either village, the chiefs began to pull harder. Ananse felt himself being pulled apart. When the feasts were over, the chiefs set out to find out what had happened to Ananse. They found him nearly dead. They untied the ropes, and Ananse was so ashamed of his greediness that he ran away and hid.

ARCHITECTURE

Each tribe has its own version of private houses and meeting houses. The secret societies also build places for their meetings. The Sande meeting places are plain, while the Poro huts are elaborately decorated. Ordinary houses are painted in geometric designs by women and pictorial designs by men. Kpelle houses are, by tradition, rectangular, with their outer walls decorated and a little covered porch area in one corner. Gio huts are circular, with a high mud platform around the base, into which the roof supports are embedded. Bassa huts are rectangular, with a long porch along the front.

The settlers built houses based on 19th century houses from Virginia and the Carolinas. Public buildings of the early period were Georgian in style, while in the 1920s a kind of Afro-Brazilian style became popular. In the 1950s, during an economic upturn, many public buildings were designed by European architects in a modern style. Under the rule of Samuel Doe, some very grand marble and glass buildings were erected.

The National Culture Center in Kendeja displays the architecture of 16 ethnic groups of Liberia.

MUSIC

Music is a vital part of daily life in Liberia. In tribal society rhythm is a basic accompaniment to most activities—rowing boats, sowing seeds, cutting plants, building houses. Funerals, births, and war all call for different songs. Today the gospel music of the churches fills the airwaves, and collections of traditional songs have been modernized.

Traditional music has a distinctive sound because of the instruments used. Various types of xylophone are common, often with gourds hanging below them to create a resonance. Rattles of all kinds, made out of anything from gourds to tin cans, are also used, as well as various string

The Kru are famous for their choirs that sing in a complex series of harmonies.

Music is an essential component of life in Liberia, both rural and urban.

instruments. These might be simple lutes—made from a gourd with horsehair strings—or, in modern times, acoustic guitars. Bells, clappers, horns, and, of course, drums make up the orchestra. The most important aspect of Liberian music is rhythm rather than melody. As in all West African music, drums and other percussion instruments are used to set up complex beat patterns, with different rhythms overlaying one another.

Modern Liberian music has borrowed from this tradition and also from the "Highlife" big band music of Ghana and Sierra Leone, a dance style that emerged in the 1950s using African rhythms alongside regimental band music, Latin American rhythms, and West Indian calypso music. As soon as recording became possible in Liberia, in the 1920s, collections of Liberian music began featuring a female Vai singer called Zondogbo. Later, during World War II, there were many Americans stationed in Liberia; their music came with them and influenced local styles.

The effort to collect traditional music was greatest in the 1960s, when singers such as Zuke Kiazolu and Zina Zoldoa were recorded. Two radio stations, ELBC and ELWA, broadcast popular songs daily and sent researchers out to the rural areas to collect new folk songs.

In modern Liberia, Americo-Liberian music is largely gospel style. Popular music has suffered the effects of the civil war. Local music is available only on bootleg cassette tapes and is either linked with American soul/funk music, as in the tapes of Dave or Big Steve Worjloh, or is more West African in style, as in the music of Gbesa Body, who plays folk guitar.

A Gio man plays one of Liberia's many traditional string instruments.

A LIVING ART AND CRAFT

Art as an essential part of daily tribal life can be seen in the elaborate masks used in tribal festivals and religious rituals, as well as in the costumes designed for them. Although they were considered sacred objects, the masks were given away to anthropologists—in an effort to preserve them—by tribal leaders who saw their traditions being lost in the move to westernize Liberian society.

The masks are made of sapwood and often have steel or aluminum teeth. They are usually brightly painted with dyes collected from indigenous plants and can be beautiful or fierce looking depending on their purpose. One type of mask has an elongated beak, while another has tubular protruding eyes and a horn on its forehead.

Today, replicas of these masks are made for cultural purposes and as craft objects. Woodcarvers make figures from ebony, camwood, cherry, walnut, and mahogany. The Kissi carve figures from soapstone, while the Grebo make clay models. Dan artists cast jewelry in bronze or brass using the lost wax method.

In times happier than those of the last decade, modern art flourished in Monrovia, with galleries displaying the paintings and sculptures of local artists. The National Museum was looted during the civil war, but a collection of masks and ceramics survives at the Cuttington University College.

Among the Americo-Liberian community, painting and sculpture began only in the mid-20th century and were largely religious in nature. In the 1960s a Liberian school of artists emerged, many of them trained in Europe,

Masks are far more than decorative objects—in the Sande and Poro cults, especially, they are believed to be the embodiment of the power they represented. Many such masks were collected in the middle of the 20th century by anthropologists.

and by the 1970s regular exhibitions were being held. After the 1990 coup two prominent artists, Jallah Kollie and Vanjah Richards, were killed, and a third, Cietta Mensah, left for the United States. Richards, a sculptor and painter, was commissioned before the coup to paint scenes of Liberian history and mythology for several large hotels and public buildings. Painters who have remained in Liberia and survived the fighting are Wantue Major, who focuses on graphic images of the horror of war, Omar al Shabu, and Winston Richards, an abstract expressionist.

Craftwork from Liberia includes masks, figures carved from wood and ivory in designs taken from the totems of indigenous religions, woven mats and baskets, cloth, gold and silver jewelry, and musical instruments. Dru, a woodcarver from Liberia, has found fame with exhibitions of his work in the United States.

When the Carthaginian explorer Hanno landed on what is thought to be Liberian soil in the fifth century B.C., he recorded that he and his men spent a sleepless night listening to the sound of drumming coming from the jungle around them. It convinced them to leave the next morning.

The *sowei* ("SOH-way") or *zogbei* ("ZOG-bay"), a mask in the shape of a helmet that covers the entire head, is used in Sande rituals. It is unique in that it is the only mask used and owned solely by women.

LEISURE

BEFORE THE CIVIL WAR drove expatriate workers out of Liberia and sent half the population into refugee camps outside its borders, leisure activities in the country could be classified into three main types. In the cities there were a variety of urban leisure facilities, such as movie theaters, art galleries, clubs, discos, and sporting facilities and events, some of which have survived the war. Films continue to be very popular, with about 1.5 million people going to the movies every year. In the inner city of Monrovia and in the mining and agricultural concessions run by foreign companies there were clubs, restaurants, and sporting facilities for the expatriate workers. In the rural areas the long post-harvest period was when villagers had the time and money to relax and enjoy the dancing and singing of their numerous festivals. At other times they enjoyed just relaxing in a hammock under the trees.

Opposite: **One of the entertainment attractions on a Monrovian street. A stilt dancer draws out the crowds.**

Left: **In the towns both Western and African styles of dancing are in vogue, but in the villages traditional rhythms are favored.**

The markets in small towns are different from those in the cities, with unusual animals being sold for food and medicine, as well as herbs collected from the forest, charms, and talismans.

LEISURE IN THE CITIES

Monrovia is a small and poor city by Western standards. It has been considerably damaged by the fighting. However, in times of relative peace its citizens can choose from a range of leisure pursuits. There are movie theaters, although there is no Liberian film industry. Chinese kung-fu films are very popular. There are cafés, known locally as cookshops, where simple Liberian food can be eaten, as well as more upmarket restaurants for an evening out. Clubs and discos, a few with satellite TV and some with live music, have a charged atmosphere. Churchgoers often have their own organized functions, and the tribal associations also have meeting places and organize activities. Markets are a popular leisure spot for people who shop daily for groceries, household goods, and cloth. There are a few Western-style supermarkets selling mostly imported foods.

In the smaller towns there are frequent power cuts, so evening diversions are limited to the nights when there is electricity.

RURAL LEISURE ACTIVITIES

Rural life in Liberia consists of work, leisure, festivals, and the arts. Until the harvest most people have little time for leisure pursuits, but when it is over many men plan a hunting trip, partly for food and partly for the pleasure of the hunt. Pipe smoking is a popular way of relaxing among both men and women. So is drinking palm wine in the evenings, with a kola nut as a chaser. A popular leisure game played all over Africa is called *mancala* ("man-KAH-lah"). It is a little like checkers and is played on a 2- to 3-foot wooden boat-shaped board with hollows for the counters.

Talk dominates in the workplace and at the fireside. Liberians have a long tradition of recording their history and beliefs in epic tales that help pass on their values to succeeding generations. These values are evident even on informal family evenings, when conversations are peppered with stories, proverbs, and cautionary tales.

Two Dan villagers enjoy a quiet game of *mancala.* The object is to go around the board, taking as many of the opponent's counters as possible while protecting one's own.

LEISURE FOR EXPATRIATES

Most foreigners in Liberia were evacuated by their governments in 1990, and few have been able to return. A few missionaries and aid workers have ventured back into the country, but the large expatriate work force has yet to return. When there were expatriates in the country, their leisure needs were catered for by clubs, TV bars, private swimming pools, and expensive restaurants. Yekepa, the second largest town in Liberia, is a big iron concession town. Before the civil war it doubled as a highland resort for wealthy Liberians and expatriates. The town has many sports facilities, including an Olympic-size pool and a golf course, the only one in the world that straddles two countries (Liberia and Guinea).

Expatriates in Monrovia frequented the Hotel Africa, with its lawns, swimming pool, and upscale restaurants.

A Liberian soccer team. Soccer is the most popular sport in the country.

SPORTS

The most popular sport in Liberia is association soccer, which is the type of soccer played in Europe. An intercounty competition is held for the championship every year. Local teams play in a national association, and Liberia plays in an African league. Its national team has been relatively successful in the preliminary matches for the forthcoming World Cup competition.

Other sports that are popular, particularly in the cities, include basketball, swimming, and squash, although swimming pools and squash courts tend to be in expatriate clubs. Liberia has a national basketball team. Schoolchildren enjoy playing kickball, a game similar to baseball. It is played on the same diamond-shaped court, with a pitcher and home runs, but the ball is kicked rather than hit with a bat. Another children's game is like marbles, often played with dried seeds. Four marbles (or seeds) are stacked in a pyramid on the ground, and players flick their own marbles toward it in order to knock it down. The first to do so wins the marbles.

THE MEDIA

In the city there is electricity for most of the day and television for a few hours daily. Television has not yet become a major part of people's lives, chiefly because of the expense of the equipment. There is only one television station, which is state-owned, and TV broadcasts can be picked up only in Monrovia. Radios are more widely used, and there are several radio stations, including Voice of America. The BBC World Service as well as a Sudanese station can be picked up in Liberia. Until 1990 there were many vocal newspapers, but since then there has been tight press control. Few foreign newspapers are available. Five dailies are published in Liberia, although they are small because of the fighting in Monrovia— *Inquirer, Daily Observer, Democrat, Monrovia Daily News,* and *National Chronicle.* A regional journal called *West Africa Magazine* was banned in Liberia from 1985 to 1990 because of its criticism of the government.

Political news dominates the press and accounts for newspapers often changing their names as new political groups emerge. Here a group in Monrovia reads about the dawn of a new age in the *New Liberian* **in 1980.**

GAMES AND SONGS

Villagers enliven many of their activities with song. Cradle songs are an example of the use of music in daily life. Songs also come into play in children's games. Among the Gola there is a game called *nenya* ("NEN-yah"). A group of children choose one child to be a grain of rice. Another child must protect the grain of rice from the other children, who are all hungry birds. The children must creep into the circle drawn around the "rice" and tag it without being tagged themselves. A tagged "bird" becomes the "rice." As they dart in and out of the circle, the children sing a song that mimics the call of the birds in the fields.

An all-boys game played by Vai children is *Mba N Ko Dende* ("MBAR ehn koh DEN-de") or "Mother Give Me a Canoe." All the children hold hands in a circle and choose one boy to be "it." He has to find a weak spot in the chain of hands and break it. As he does so he sings a song about canoes, asking if he can take the canoe. If a child in the chain answers "yes," the boy who is "it" can try to break his hold. When he succeeds, the next boy enters the circle and the game begins again.

A child gets into position for the crab game.

Children also play games similar to tag. One is known as the crab game. A line is drawn on the ground, and two teams line up along it with their hands and feet on the ground behind them a little like crabs. Only their feet are allowed to cross the line. The object is to tag one of their opponents with the foot before the opponent tags them. Those who are tagged must sit out of the game.

FESTIVALS

THREE RELIGIONS DOMINATE THE festivals of Liberia—Christianity, Islam, and animism. All have changed as they have come in contact with one another. Christian festivals, for example, have taken on a more energetic style, with drumming and colorful processions. With the spread of Islam and Christianity, local festivals are taking on a less dominant role in village society.

Falling somewhere between entertainment and festival are the many vibrant song, dance, and performance events that take place in the rural areas. The Kpelle call these events *pelee* ("PEL-ee"). Sande and Poro festivals also include vigorous celebration, dance, and other activities.

In the last decade or so of war, much of Liberian culture, including its festivals, has been disrupted to the point of extinction. A glimmer of peace has now returned to the country, and observers can only hope that the old ways of life will return with it.

In a daily ceremony, the state flag is raised at 7:45 a.m. at every school.

Opposite: **A Dan masquerade.**

Left: **Christian festivals in Liberia may include staged performances.**

Christmas is celebrated with enthusiasm in the rural areas. It coincides with the long period of leisure and celebration among villagers when the harvest is over and people have money.

Thanksgiving, a public holiday in Liberia, is a time for families to get together.

CHRISTIAN FESTIVALS

Liberian Christians celebrate the main Christian festivals, and Christmas and Easter are public holidays. There are Christian missions in every small town which celebrate the festivals with a mixture of African and Christian traditions. African churches such as the Aladura celebrate with colorful processions, music with a lively rhythm, and emotionally charged services involving miracle events like talking in tongues and faith healing. The older Baptist churches are more sedate. At Christmas, gifts are given and church bells sound. Easter is a more somber occasion, marking as it does the crucifixion and assumption of Christ.

MUSLIM FESTIVALS

Muslim festivals are not public holidays in Liberia, but they are celebrated throughout the country. Because the Muslim calendar is based on the moon's revolution around the earth rather than the earth's around the sun, the dates of Muslim festivals change every year. Ramadan, the ninth month of the Islamic calendar, is a period of fasting from dawn to dusk. In the evenings the fast is broken, and in Muslim areas the cookshops stay open and there is an atmosphere of celebration. Eid al-Fitr, the festival that marks the end of Ramadan, lasts four days from the first day of the 10th month. The family home is cleaned and new clothes are bought. Families visit one another, and great feasts are held. For Muslims this celebrates the successful end to a period of spiritual cleansing and is the most important event of the year. Eid al-Adha, the 10th day of the 12th month, celebrates Abraham's willingness to sacrifice his son. An animal is slaughtered, and meat is given to the poor.

AFRICAN FESTIVALS

Many African festivals take place in the fall, when the hard work of the year is over and the harvest is in. The Sande and Poro festivals often take place then, and the proper celebration of events such as funerals is delayed until this time, when suitable attention can be paid to them.

A man beats his drum during the Bassa farming festival which takes place in February, when the new crop is about to be sown.

One ritual with roots in the ancient ways of village people involves the *Go Ge* ("Go GAY"). When a particularly disruptive dispute occurred in a village, someone would be called in to arbitrate. This was the *Go Ge,* often the village leader wearing a disguising mask. The term is roughly translated as "Cow Devil." The *Go Ge* would arrive ceremoniously and mediate between the warring parties. At the resolution of the problem, a cow would be sacrificed by the loser and a feast would be held.

THE WOI EPIC

Festivals are often an occasion for bringing the professional storyteller into the village for a performance involving music, storytelling, dance, and mime. The stories are often epic poems that exist only in the memories of the storytellers, just as the *Iliad* and *Odyssey* once were.

One well-recorded example of this is a Kpelle myth called the Woi epic, a complicated story about a superhuman hero called Woi. The naughty spider is in the story, as are several objects that are personified, such as Woi's house, bow, ax, and cutlass. Woi's bull has been stolen by Yele Lawo, a monster spirit, and Woi has to go to battle. Many adventures and fights beset Woi and his allies as he tries to move his house into the sky.

The storyteller organizes a chorus that sings in between episodes of the story. When it is trained, he turns to persons in the audience and makes them the questioners or *mar kee ke nuu* ("mar KEY kay new"). They call out questions about the events, to give the storyteller the links to the next part of the story and provide a feedback that everyone understands. Finally the whole audience is organized into sections, all singing or chanting or playing (tapping on drums and bottles) at different rhythms at the same time. If a section of the audience makes a mistake, the storyteller can call on another section and get the rhythm and story going again.

As he tells the story the storyteller sits up on his knees, using his arms as a shadow play of events, the lanterns and torches around him creating a larger-than-life figure. The story has no beginning and no end. The storyteller can begin with an episode that suits the evening's performance, and he carries on until all the episodes are told. It is unlikely that this epic is written down anywhere or even recorded, and so as the older generation dies out and the younger people go off to the towns, chances are that Woi's epic will be lost for all time.

WEDDINGS

Most tribal weddings are grand celebrations, with performances by professional dance troupes, a great feast, and gift giving. These ceremonies often end with a procession of the newlyweds and their friends to the groom's village.

Among the Kpelle, however, weddings are a very low-key, if not quite secret, business. What is important in Kpelle weddings is the acknowledgment by the head of the family that the union is official. A Kpelle wedding involves the tribal elders giving the newlyweds advice about marital responsibilities. The couple's relatives attend and must give assurances that they will intervene in any marital disputes. A small token is given by the groom's relatives to the bride's, and the woman is ceremoniously handed over to the man. Bride wealth negotiations are settled, and then the ritual is over.

CALENDAR OF PUBLIC HOLIDAYS

January 1	New Year's Day
February 11	Armed Forces Day
Second Wednesday in March	Decoration Day
March 15	J.J. Roberts' Birthday
Second Friday in April	Prayer and Fast Day
Variable	Easter Friday
Variable	Easter Sunday
July 26	National Independence Day
First Thursday in November	Thanksgiving Day
November 29	William Tubman's Birthday
December 25	Christmas

A Bassa girl in Rivercess County with the traditional body paint of a Sande initiate.

SECRET SOCIETY FESTIVALS

Secret societies are not important in modern urban life, but in rural areas it is still customary for most young men and women to undergo a period of instruction in bush schools; when they emerge they are considered adults. This event now lasts only a few weeks, to fit in with the school term, but in the past it lasted a few years. All boys and girls of a certain age are inducted into the secret society, in a ceremony that symbolizes the death of the old person. The rituals involved in the Sande and Poro ceremonies are rites of passage from childhood to adulthood. The masks and costumes of each society are kept in the society hut and may not be seen by outsiders. They completely cover the wearer, who is often the highest ranking member of the society. In one Poro ceremony each boy is completely swallowed up by the masked figure, who wears a huge straw costume. This signifies the death of the boy. Other rituals act out the impaling of the boy. When he returns to his family he is supposed to be a different person.

Another ritual, called "breaking the bush," returns the new person to his family, and there is a joyful celebration involving dancing, feasting, and music. The boy puts on the tribal gown, in many cases a long embroidered shirt. In the graduation festival for girls they become the chief performers in the dancing and singing, and at the end of the festival they are judged on how well they have learned the skills taught. Parents exchange gifts with their children. The event ends with the ritual putting on of a woman's *lappas*, headdress, and beads.

BIRTH RITUALS

There are songs and rituals associated with childbirth in rural Liberia. Tribes that have secret societies often have a special house for childbirth, where Sande women help in the delivery. Childbirth is still risky in Liberia, and a successful delivery is accompanied by dances and songs to protect the child and its mother. If the child is related to the village chief, the celebrations are very grand.

FUNERAL CELEBRATION

Like other aspects of Liberian life, the complex rituals associated with burying the dead have altered with the war and the influence of Islam and Christianity. Modern funeral rituals often involve both African songs and Christian hymns or Islamic chants.

The funeral procession of a Bassa *zoe*.

Traditional funeral ceremonies, especially among tribes with Sande and Poro societies, often lasted many days. The body was held for three or four days under the eaves of the palaver hut. On those days the men of the Dei tribe would dance the *ziawa* ("zee-AH-wah"), called *gbaa* ("geh-BAH") in some languages, while the women stayed indoors. When a Sande *zoe* died, similar songs and dances were performed for three days. Although many of these ceremonies are now rare, some of the songs have been recorded.

The festival to celebrate the death of a chief is a big affair. It might take up to two years to prepare for, and when it does take place it includes the celebration for the new chief. The long period of preparation is to give the family time to save for the enormous cost of the celebration. A cow must be killed, neighboring chiefs are invited, and fine clothes and accomplished dancers must be found.

Decoration Day marks the day when people of various religions go to the graveyards to decorate and tidy the family graves.

111

FOOD

LIBERIAN FOOD HAS SIMILARITIES with other West African cuisines, in which cassava root and rice are the staples of most meals. In Liberia, though, there is the long tradition of cooking brought to the country by the Americo-Liberians as well as the influence of Western expatriates.

STAPLES

Both types of rice, wet and dry, can be grown in Liberia without the complex irrigation systems that are used in other countries. Rice and cassava are grown in every rural household and sold in the city markets.

Cassava is an edible root that is poor in nutrients but thrives in the damp climate of Liberia. It has the advantage that it can be left in the ground until it is needed. Other starchy foods grown in the country include *eddoes* (taro, an edible root), plantains, sweetcorn, and sweet potatoes. The pulp of palm nuts is also an important staple in the Liberian diet.

Opposite: **Palm nuts form an important staple of the Liberian diet. The nuts are pounded into a pulp and cooked into a sauce called palm butter.**

Left: **Unusual and interesting foods can be bought in the village market.**

MEAT

In Liberia game is now hunted with guns, but in the old days bows and arrows were used.

Meat is a luxury in the villages, with hunting and fishing the main sources of supply. Game includes antelope, wild pigs, and even leopards, while other sources of protein are lizards, snakes, frogs, termites, and snails. Smaller animals are caught in traps. A common practice is for women and children to go down to the river, where the children get into the water and make a noise to frighten the fish downstream. The women wait for the fish with small nets and trap them as they move away from the noise. When men fish in the streams, they use a hook and line or poison a pool with sasswood bark. This stuns the fish but does not make them poisonous to eat. Fish are eaten fresh or dried. Chickens are kept but are saved for their eggs and for sacrifices, and goat is a popular meat in the cities. Cattle are a luxury and are slaughtered only for important festivals.

ANANSE AND THE FRUIT OF THE FOREST

One day Ananse the spider decided to accompany a village girl as she looked for food in the forest. She was a good gatherer and knew all the best secret places to find good things to eat. First she went to where there was a small fruit tree with a few ripe fruit. Ananse pushed past her and ate them all up. The girl sighed and went to the next place she knew, a banana grove with small but sweet bananas. Ananse grabbed them all and ate them up again.

The girl got irritated with Ananse and decided to teach him a lesson. She took him deep into the bush, where she knew there was a colony of honey bees inside a tree stump. She showed Ananse the big combs of honey, and although he was really full with fruit he jumped inside the stump and started eating. Soon he was swollen with honey, and when he tried to get out of the tree stump he found he was stuck. "Help me," he cried, "I can't get out."

"Not likely," said the girl and went off to where she knew there were some huge cassavas that she could dig up for her family. Ananse called for help, but he was deep in the forest where no one could hear him.

OTHER FOODS

Liberia has many types of fresh produce. A wide variety of vegetables are grown in kitchen gardens including cucumber, okra, collard greens, lima beans, and cabbage. Onions, *eddoes*, chili peppers, coconuts, ginger, eggplants, tomatoes, and other vegetables thrive in the Liberian climate. Sweet potato leaves and cassava leaves are boiled and eaten as vegetables, while cassava is prepared in a traditional, labor-intensive way—by soaking and pounding it before cooking.

Fruit is also plentiful and includes soursop, grapefruit, mangoes, oranges, pineapples, bananas, and watermelons. Peanuts are used in baking cakes and cookies as well as in a savory sauce. Also in the kitchen garden are kola trees. The kola nut is of no value as a food, but it is chewed as a stimulant because of its caffeine content.

Above and below: **Chili peppers and bananas thrive in Liberia's equatorial climate.**

A TYPICAL MEAL

Bug a bug, or termites, are eaten raw or roasted in Liberia.

Rice is normally eaten boiled, with a spicy sauce that may contain meat. Sometimes it is cooked into a kind of risotto called *jollof,* with meat and vegetables. A seasonal alternative to rice is cassava, cooked into a porridge with other vegetables and meat, or made into little boat-shaped cakes that are used to scoop up the accompanying stew. Other common dishes are *fufu* ("FOO-foo"), a fermented cassava porridge, and *dumboy* ("DUM-boy"), the unfermented version. These are served with palm butter and vegetables. *Tumborgee* ("tum-BOR-gee"), or fermented palm butter, is common in Lofa. Palm butter and *tumborgee* are served more as a stew than a sauce and often contain meat, beans, onions, or vegetables in season. Frog soup is quite common, and deep-fried vegetables, fish, and termites (called *bug a bug*) are popular.

Children at a feeding center in Monrovia eat their ration of rice and beans distributed by the UN World Food Program.

A LIBERIAN FEAST

In a Liberian feast all the dishes are set out together. Nothing is cleared away during the meal, and no new dishes are brought in. The centerpiece may be a roasted animal. *Dumboy* and *fufu* form the base of the meal. With them are palm butter, palaver sauce (a meat stew made with spinach leaves), or *tumborgee*. Goat soup and "check rice" (rice and okra) are also served. Meat dishes might be pig trotters with cabbage, fish with sweet potato leaves, and shrimp with palm nuts. Fried plantains and organ soup, the national dishes, are likely to be present. Vegetable dishes include Monrovian collards and cabbage cooked in a soup with bacon, chili, and onions. Dessert may be fruit, cakes, rice bread, or sweet potato pone. In a village feast, utensils consist of spoons, bowls, and plates. In a city feast, there are Western utensils with glasses and a place setting for each guest.

Women carry firewood on their heads to the kitchen, in preparation for a communal feast.

EATING OUT

All over Liberia there are small eating places known as cookshops. Country chop, their most famous dish, consists of meat, fish, and greens fried in palm oil. In the markets, street stalls sell deep-fried foods and cooked seafood. In Monrovia the dining establishments range from cookshops to gourmet restaurants serving French or Italian cuisine. Somewhere between the two are US-influenced restaurants serving hamburgers, American breakfasts, and fried chicken alongside Liberian dishes such as *bong* fries (fried cassava chips).

A strong Lebanese influence can be seen in the many small Lebanese restaurants selling hummus, *fuul* ("FU-ul"), *khobez* ("KOH-bez," Lebanese bread), and pastries such as baklava. Indian restaurants are also numerous in the cities. Another import from the West is the many pastry shops selling cookies, cakes, chocolate, and ice cream. A popular local cake is Monrovian coconut pie, made with grated coconut meat, milk, and eggs. Many local ice creams are available, made with fresh fruit, eggs, and milk.

BEVERAGES

Popular drinks in Liberia are bottled beer made in Monrovia, palm wine made from fermented palm fruit, ginger beer, and a rum made from sugarcane. Milk is rarely drunk, and coffee drinking is an urban custom.

Palm wine is made by collecting the sap from palm trees. It is left in a calabash—a hollowed-out gourd hardened in the sun—where natural yeasts collect on it. Fermentation is rapid. The drink is first very sweet and fizzy, then it turns alcoholic, and in two weeks it becomes a sour wine. It is a valuable village produce, and some people keep many palm trees for this purpose. Palm wine is an essential part of celebrations and public village meetings. It can be used as currency, as part payment of bride price, and as taxes paid to a chief. A kola nut is often sucked while palm wine is drunk, since kola acts as a stimulant and is said to keep the head clear.

A woman sells home-made drinks in recycled bottles.

KITCHEN EQUIPMENT

In the villages the basic means of cooking is an open fire outside the hut at the back of the building. The hearth is made of three flat stones, with the fire inside. A large iron cooking pot rests on the stones. Equipment for stirring the food is made locally from wood and is rarely bought or made of metal.

A large log of wood is fashioned into an hourglass shape and hollowed out to provide a container for pounding cassava with a thick wooden pole. Covers for food are woven from palm fiber or, in the bigger towns, are made of plastic. Fishing nets, another vital piece of equipment, are also made from palm fiber. Plastic buckets and enamel bowls are often part of a dowry, and the iron cooking pot is an object of great value.

When water is collected a long distance from the village, a rod is held across the shoulders to balance two containers. The traditional container is a calabash, but sometimes buckets are used.

Every piece of kitchen equipment is treasured, and very few things are thrown away. Empty produce cans are reused as cooking pots, while glass jars are a rare luxury. If a woman divorces her husband she takes her cooking utensils with her, because they represent her real wealth.

At mealtime, most people use either their hands or a carved wooden spoon. At big feasts there are no dishes—each person helps themselves from the common dishes—but at home the food is distributed into bowls when the meal starts. The bowls are either made at home out of wood or are made of the more precious plastic or enamel and bought from the market.

In the cities the degree of sophistication of the kitchen varies enormously—from fairly modern gas stoves and refrigerators in the houses of the very rich, to charcoal fires outside the house, often in a little open-roofed hut separate from the main building. A butane gas cylinder is a sign of a well-to-do family, as are drinking glasses, factory-made plates, and metal knives and forks.

Opposite: **A girl pounds wheat to prepare** *kala***, a deep-fried dish she will later sell at the market.**

LIBERIAN RICE BREAD

This delicious rice bread stays moist for a week and serves six people.

2 cups Cream of Rice cereal (ground rice)
4 tablespoons sugar
3 cups mashed banana
$1/2$ cup vegetable oil
1 teaspoon salt
$1/2$ teaspoon nutmeg
1 teaspoon baking powder

1. Combine all the ingredients in a bowl and mix well.
2. Grease a 9-inch (23 cm) round cake tin.
3. Pour the mixture into the pan and bake in a preheated oven at 400°F (240°C) for 30 minutes. Test if the bread is done by inserting a wooden skewer. If it comes out clean, then the bread is ready.
4. Remove the bread from the tin and place it on a rack to cool.

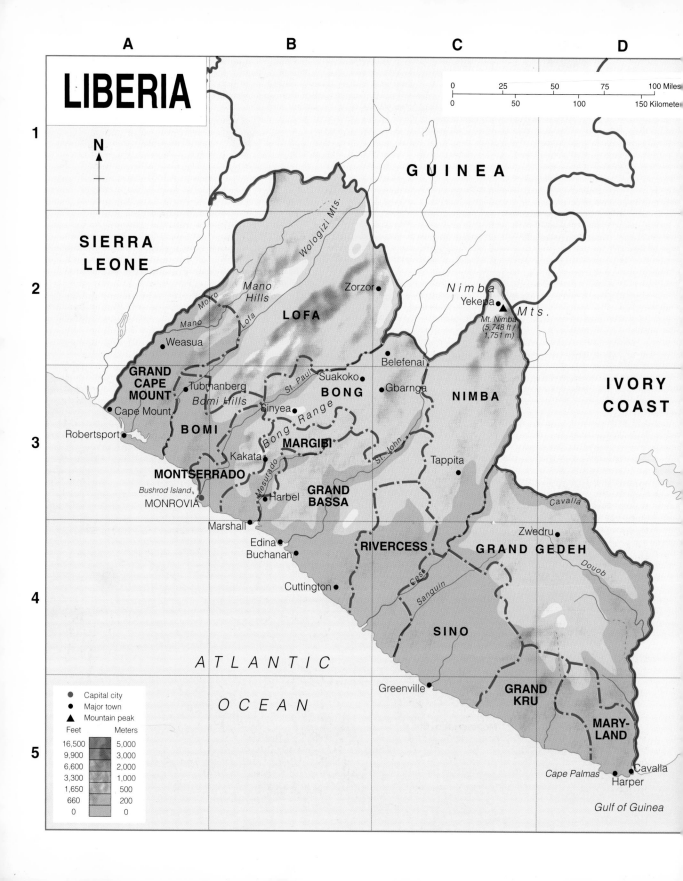

Atlantic Ocean, B4	Greenville, C5	Rivercess, C4	Tappita, C3
	Guinea, C1	Robertsport, A3	Tubmanberg, A3
Belefenai, C2	Gulf of Guinea, D5		
Bomi, A3		Sanguin River, C4	Weasua, A2
Bomi Hills, A3	Harbel, B3	Sierra Leone, A2	Wologizi Mountains, B2
Bong, B3	Harper, D5	Sino, C4	
Bong Range, B3		Sinyea, B3	Yekepa, C2
Buchanan, B4	Ivory Coast, D3	St. John River, C3	
Bushrod Island, A3		St. Paul River, B3	Zorzor, C2
	Kakata, B3	Suakoko, B3	Zwedru, D4
Cape Mount, A3			
Cape Palmas, D5	Lofa, B2		
Cavalla, D5	Lofa River, B2		
Cavalla River, D3			
Cess River, C4	Mano Hills, B2		
Cuttington, B4	Mano River, A2		
	Margibi, B3		
Douobé River, D4	Marshall, B4		
	Maryland, D5		
Edina, B4	Mesurado River, B3		
	Monrovia, A3		
Gbarnga, C3	Montserrado, B3		
Grand Cape Mount, A3	Morro River, A2		
Grand Bassa, B3			
Grand Gedeh, C4	Nimba, C3		
Grand Kru, C5	Nimba, Mt., C2		
	Nimba Mountains, C2		

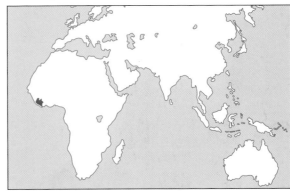

QUICK NOTES

OFFICIAL NAME
Republic of Liberia

FIRST GOVERNOR
Thomas Buchanan

HEAD OF STATE
President Charles Taylor

POPULATION
3 million

LAND AREA
43,000 square miles (111,370 sq km)

CAPITAL
Monrovia

MAJOR TOWNS
Buchanan, Edina, Greenville, Harper, Marshall, Robertsport, Yekepa

ADMINISTRATIVE DISTRICTS (COUNTIES)
Bomi, Bong, Grand Bassa, Grand Cape Mount, Grand Gedeh, Grand Kru, Lofa, Margibi, Maryland, Montserrado, Nimba, Rivercess, Sino

HIGHEST POINT
Mt. Nimba at Guest House Hill
(5,748 ft/1,751 m)

GROSS NATIONAL PRODUCT (GNP)
US$2 billion

GNP PER CAPITA
Approximately US$700

MAJOR RIVERS
St. Paul, Lofa

LANGUAGES
English; 30 or more indigenous languages

RELIGIONS
Christianity, Islam, animism

CURRENCY
Liberian dollar (officially equivalent to the US$)

EXPORTS
Rubber, coffee, and iron ore

IMPORTS
Processed food

NATIONAL HOLIDAY
Independence Day, July 26

NATIONAL FLAG
Eleven equal horizontal stripes of red alternating with white; a white five-pointed star on a blue square in upper hoist corner.

NATIONAL SYMBOL
Heraldic shield with dove of peace carrying an open scroll. The crest bears the motto "The Love of Liberty Brought Us Here." Below the motto is a ship and sunrise; in the foreground is land with a palm tree, plow, and spade.

TRIBES
Bassa, Belle, Dei, Gbandi, Gio, Gola, Grebo, Kissi, Kpelle, Krahn, Kru, Loma, Mandingo, Mano, Mende, Vai

GLOSSARY

Aladura ("AL-ad-ER-ah")
An African Christian church.

Ananse ("ah-NAN-say")
Spider that figures in African stories.

calabash ("KAL-ah-bash")
Container made from hollowed-out gourd.

Congo ("KON-goh")
People descended from freed slaves.

Creole ("KREE-ol")
Language that amalgamates two others.

dumboy ("DUM-boy")
Unfermented cassava porridge.

fufu ("FOO-foo")
Fermented cassava porridge.

Go Ge ("go GAY")
Arbiter of village disputes.

Krio ("KREE-oh")
Creole language spoken in Sierra Leone.

kwi ("KWEE")
Pidgin English for "foreigner."

Malinke ("mah-LINK-ee")
Language spoken by the Mandingo.

mancala ("man-KAH-lah")
Board game played with counters.

mar kee ke nuu ("mar KEY kay new")
Questioner in the audience during a Woi epic.

nenya ("NEN-yah")
Gola children's game.

palaver hut ("puh-LAV-er hut")
Place where village councils meet.

pelee ("PEL-ee")
Music, dance, and performance festival.

Poro ("POH-roh")
Male secret society.

saa saa ("SAH sah")
Rattle made from a gourd and some beads.

Sande ("SAN-day")
Female secret society.

syllabary ("SIL-uh-bur-ee")
A kind of alphabet consisting of a character for each combination of vowel and consonant, or syllable.

to nuu ("toh NEW")
Rich and powerful African leader. Translates into English as "big shot."

tumborgee ("tum-BOR-gee")
Fermented palm butter.

zoe ("ZOH")
Priest, usually head of Poro or Sande society.

BIBLIOGRAPHY

Ayo, Yvonne. *Eyewitness Guides: Africa.* London: Dorling Kindersley, 1995.

Cordor, S. Henry, editor. *New Voices from West Africa. An anthology of Liberian Stories.* Monrovia: Books for Africa Press, 1980.

Liberia in Pictures. Lerner Visual Geography Series. Minneapolis: Lerner, 1988.

Nelson, Harold B. *Liberia: A Country Study.* Washington: The American University, 1985.

Schuman, Edythe Rance Haskett Abelard. *Grains of Pepper: Folktales from Liberia.* London: 1970.

INDEX

Abuja Accord, 29
agriculture, 24, 39, 40, 42, 49, 61, 97
airport, 13, 44
Aladura, 76, 106
American Colonization Society, 19, 22, 23
Americo-Liberians, 27, 31, 32, 47, 52, 53, 55, 60, 71, 81, 88, 93, 94, 113
ancestor worship, 72
animism, 71–4, 105
architecture, 58–9, 91
Ashmun, Jehudi, 22, 75
Atlantic Ocean, 7, 8, 13, 22, 41

Barclay, Arthur, 34
Barclay, Edwin, 25, 34
Bassa, 20, 47, 50, 52, 68, 71, 76, 82, 83, 91, 107, 110, 111
Belle, 47, 50, 52, 82
"big shots," 67, 81
birds, 14, 15
birthrate, 49
birth rituals, 111
Body, Gbesa, 93
Bomi (county), 35
Brazil, 24
bride price, 36, 66–7, 109, 119
Britain, 23, 24

British, 21
Brown, Robert, 88
bubba, 54
Buchanan, 9, 44, 48
Buchanan, Thomas, 23
bug a bug, 116
Bukele, Dualu, 84
Bushrod Island, 13, 26

cacao, 39, 42
calabash, 119, 120
Cape Mesurado, 13, 75
Cape Mount, 12
cassava, 42, 65, 113, 115, 116, 118, 120
Catholic Church, 75
Cavalla, 43
children, 52, 66, 90, 103, 110
Christianity, 52, 65, 71, 73, 75–7, 88, 105, 106, 111
Christmas, 106
civil war, 3, 28, 29, 31, 33, 34, 36, 37, 40, 44, 47, 53, 55, 60, 63, 93, 94, 97, 100, 105
climate, 12, 113, 115
cocoa, 24
coconut palm, 43, 57
coffee, 7, 10, 11, 17, 24, 39, 42, 51, 119
Congoes, 52
constitution, 31, 53
cookshop, 98, 107, 118

Cooper, Charles, 89
Corker, R. Sylvanus, 89
Council of State, 31, 33, 34
crab game, 103
craft, 51, 62, 94–5
Cuffee, Paul, 19, 22, 23
currency, 39, 58
Cuttington University College, 61, 75, 94

Dan (Gio), 20, 34, 36, 99, 105
dancing, 51, 97, 105, 111
de Sintra, Pedro, 21
debt, 39
Dei, 20, 47, 50, 52, 82, 83, 111
diamonds, 7, 39, 41
dining customs, 121
diseases, 62–3
Doe, Samuel, 27, 28, 31, 33, 34, 57, 74, 75, 81, 91
dress, 54, 110
drinks, 119
Dru, 95
drums, 85, 95
dumboy, 116, 117

Easter, 106
ECOMOG, 28
Economic Community of West African States (ECOWAS), 28

INDEX

Edina, 48
education, 60–1, 79, 80
Eid al-Adha, 107
Eid al-Fitr, 107
elections, 28, 29
environmental issues, 15
Episcopal Church, 75

Fanti, 53
fauna, 14–15
Firestone Tire and Rubber
    Company, 16, 25, 26, 43
fishing, 41, 51, 53, 65, 114
flag, 22, 33
flora, 16–17
folktales, 87, 90, 114
football, 101
forestry, 39
France, 23, 39
French, 21
fruit, 115
fufu, 116, 117

Gbandi, 51, 52, 77, 82
Gbarnga, 28, 44, 77
Germany, 26, 39
Ghana, 20, 53, 76, 93
Gibson, Garretson Wilmot, 34
Gio (Dan), 20, 28, 51, 72, 82, 87,
    91, 93
Go Ge, 107
Gola, 51, 52, 77, 82, 103
gold, 41, 95
Grain Coast, 21, 22, 85
Grand Bassa (county), 35
Grand Cape Mount (county), 35,
    80
Grand Gedeh (county), 35
Grand Kru (county), 35
Grebo, 20, 50, 52, 75, 82, 94
Greenville, 23, 48
Guest House Hill, 11
Guinea, 7, 8, 10, 11, 17, 25, 29, 45,
    48, 50, 51, 82, 100
Gulf of Guinea, 8

Hanno, 21, 95
Harbel, 43
harmattan, 12

Harper, 23, 48, 55, 61, 71
health issues, 62–3
housing, 58–9, 64–5, 91
Howard, Daniel Edward, 34
hydroelectricity, 8, 41

independence, 23, 24, 109
infant mortality, 49, 63
initiation rites, 68–9, 110
iron ore, 7, 10, 13, 27, 41, 44, 45
Islam, 65, 71, 73, 77, 105, 107, 111; *see
    also* Muslims
Italy, 39
Ivory Coast, 7, 8, 10, 11, 20, 50, 82

Japan, 26
Johnson, Prince, 28
jollof, 116

Kakata, 44
kickball, 101
King, Charles Dunbar, 34
Kissi, 20, 47, 51, 52, 77, 82, 94
Kissi money, 51
kitchen equipment, 120
kola nut, 17, 51, 99, 115, 119
Kollie, Jallah, 95
Kpelle, 20, 51, 52, 59, 66, 67, 73, 75,
    76, 82, 84, 87, 91, 105, 108, 109
Krahn, 20, 28, 50, 52, 75, 82
Kru, 20, 50, 52, 59, 65, 75, 76, 79, 82,
    87, 92
Kuwaa, 82

languages:
    English, 61, 79–81, 83
    Fulani, 82
    Gbee, 83
    Kwa, 50, 79, 82
    Malinke, 83
    Mande, 20, 50, 79, 82
    West Atlantic (Mel), 51, 79, 82
lappas, 54, 110
latex, 16–17, 25, 43
law, 37, 68
League of Nations, 25
Lebanese, 13, 53, 77, 118
leopards, 14, 15, 73, 114
Liberian Assemblies of God, 76

Liberian Baptist Convention, 75
Liberian mongoose, 15
life expectancy, 49
literature, 87–9
lizards, 14, 114
Lofa (county), 60
Loma, 51, 52, 59, 75, 82, 84
Lutheran Church, 59, 75, 84

mackerel, 41, 85
magic, 68, 74
Mali, 20, 50, 82
manatee, 14
mancala, 99
Mandingo, 20, 28, 51, 52, 65, 71,
    77, 82, 83
mangrove, 9
Mano, 20, 28, 51, 82
Margibi (county), 35
markets, 65, 98, 113
marriage, 36, 52, 66–7, 68, 84, 109
Marshall, 48
Maryland (county), 35
masks, 94–5, 107, 110
Masonic Lodge, 69
Mauritania, 20
media, 102
meleguetta pepper, 21, 85
Mende, 51, 52, 77, 82, 84
Mensah, Cietta, 95
mineral resources, 41
mining, 7, 10, 39, 41, 44, 45, 48,
    59, 61, 97
Mitchel, Elizabeth , 88–9
Monrovia, 5, 7–9, 13, 19, 22, 25–7,
    31, 33, 35, 37, 40, 41, 44, 45,
    50, 53, 57–9, 61, 63, 69, 75, 81–3,
    88, 94, 97, 98, 100, 102, 116, 118,
    119
Montserrado (county), 35, 48
mountains:
    Bomi Hills, 45
    Bong Range, 45
    Mano Hills, 45
    Mt. Nimba, 10, 11, 45
    Nimba Mountains, 8, 10, 11
    Wologizi Mountains, 11
music, 75, 87, 92–3, 97, 105, 106,
    111

INDEX

Muslims, 20, 47, 51, 77, 106–7; *see also* Islam

National Assembly, 32
National Culture Center, 91, 108
National Patriotic Front of Liberia (NPFL), 33, 55
National Patriotic Party (NPP), 33
newspapers, 102
Nigeria, 33, 55, 76, 80
Nimba (county), 35, 83

oil palm, 42, 64
Omar al Shabu, 95
Order of the Eastern Star of Africa, 69
Organization of African Unity (OAU), 27, 29

palaver hut, 64, 111
palm butter, 43, 113, 116, 117
palm oil, 24, 118
palm wine, 43, 67, 99, 119
pelee, 105
People's Redemption Council, 27, 28, 34, 55
Perry, Ruth, 33, 34
poaching, 15
population, 7, 13, 20, 21, 47, 48, 49–53, 59, 61, 63, 72, 80, 97
Poro, 68, 91, 94, 105, 107, 110, 111
Portuguese, 21, 85
proverbs, 85, 90, 99
pygmy hippopotamus, 14–15

radio, 58, 93, 102
railway, 44
rainfall, 8, 12
rainforest, 7, 10, 14, 15, 41
refugees, 13, 28, 29, 48, 49, 57, 97
rice, 21, 27, 42, 43, 51, 113, 116, 117
Richards, Vanjah, 95
Richards, Winston, 95
Rivercess (county), 35, 110
rivers:
    Cavalla, 8, 85
    Gallinas, 85

Lofa, 8
Mano, 8
Sanguin, 85
St. John, 8, 85
St. Paul, 8, 13, 41, 85
roads, 44
Roberts, Joseph Jenkins, 23, 109
Robertsport, 48
rubber, 16–17, 24–7, 39, 43, 45, 48

saa saa, 87
Sande, 68, 91, 94, 95, 105, 107, 110, 111
Sankawulo, Wilton G.S., 34, 89
shantytowns, 58, 59
shipping, 45
Sierra Leone, 7, 8, 11, 19–21, 23, 28, 50, 51, 59, 76, 81, 82, 93
Sino (county), 35
slaves, 3, 19–22, 24, 25, 27, 36, 47, 50, 52, 75, 80, 88, 90
snakes, 14, 69, 114
sports, 101
Sri Lanka, 26
storytelling, 87, 99, 108
sugarcane, 42, 119

Taylor, Charles, 28, 29, 33, 34, 55
Teague, Hilary, 89
television, 102
Thanksgiving, 106
Tolbert, William Richard, 27, 31, 34
totems, 73, 95
traditional medicine, 74
transportation, 26, 44
tribal chief, 22, 23, 34, 35, 36, 37
True Whig Party, 32, 55
Tubman, William V.S., 26, 27, 31, 34, 55, 109
tumborgee, 116, 117

United Methodists, 75
United Nations, 25, 26, 27, 29, 116
United States, 3, 13, 19, 22–6, 31, 33, 39, 44, 52, 54, 55, 58, 60, 88, 90, 95, 118
University of Liberia, 61, 88

Vai, 20, 51, 52, 75, 77, 79, 82–4, 87, 93, 103
vegetables, 115

Weah, George, 55
Weasua, 80
West African Shield, 7
witchcraft, 68, 71, 74
Woi epic, 87, 108
World War II, 26, 44, 60, 84, 93

Yekepa, 100

zoe, 72, 74, 111
Zorzor, 51, 59